THE ART OF
FRAMING

THE ART OF
FRAMING

PIERS AND CAROLINE FEETHAM

Photography by PATRICK STEEL

Clarkson Potter / Publishers
New York

Published by Clarkson N. Potter/Publishers,
201 East 50th Street,
New York, New York 10022.
Member of the Crown Publishing Group.
Random House, Inc. New York, Toronto,
London, Sydney, Auckland.
http://www.ramdomhouse.com/

CLARKSON N. POTTER, POTTER, and
colophon are trademarks of Clarkson N.
Potter, inc.

Originally published in Great Britain by
Ryland Peters & Small in 1997.

Printed in Hong Kong
Library of Congress Cataloging-in-Publication
Data is available upon request.

ISBN 0-609-60081-8

10 9 8 7 6 5 4 3 2 1

First American edition

CONTENTS

Foreword 6

THE HISTORY OF
FRAMING 8
Introduction 10
The early centuries 12
French influence 18
British developments 22
Neoclassicism, Empire,
Regency 26
American native styles 30
Germany and Scandinavia 34
The 19th century 36
The Impressionists 40
The 20th century 44

THE ART OF FRAMING 46
Introduction 48
OIL PAINTINGS, TEMPERA,
AND ACRYLICS 50
The profile of the frame 52

Gold frames 54
Aluminum and silver
frames 58
Painted frames 60
Natural wood frames 62
Veneered and dark
wood frames 64
WORKS ON PAPER 66
Watercolors 68
Pastel paintings 74
Drawings 76
Charcoals and pen and ink
drawings 78
Cartoons and caricatures 80
Special treatments 82
Early prints 84
Artists' prints 86
Architectural
prints and maps 88
Decorative prints 90
Posters and graphic images 98
Collage and mixed media 100
Oriental work 102

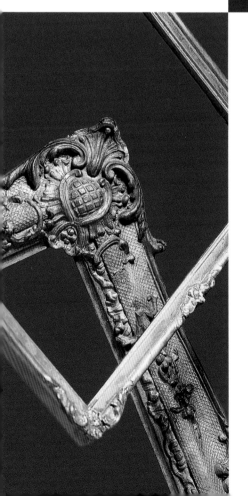

Small-scale paintings and
miniatures 104
Photographs 106
OBJECTS AND
EPHEMERA 110
Fabrics 112
Three-dimensional
objects 114
Ephemera and collections 118

THE CRAFT OF
FRAMING 122
Introduction 124
Mats 126
Mat decoration 128
Making the frame 130
Simple frame finishes 132
Decorative effects 134
Elaborate frame finishes 136
Specialized finishes 138
Gilded frames 140

Applied finishes 144
Renovating a frame 146

HANGING AND
DISPLAY 148
Introduction 150
First principles 152
Small groups 156
Regimented groups 158
The collector 160
Hanging a single picture 162
Different backgrounds 164
Combining with objects 166
Challenges 168

Credits 170
Directory of Suppliers 172
Index 174
Acknowledgments 176

FOREWORD

Our aim with this book is to share with you our fascination with the world of frames and of course the pictures and objects that go with it, and by immersing you in it, to enable you to appreciate how much can be achieved with knowledge, imagination, and flair. When we started out our concern was with the techniques of the craft. Sound craftsmanship and meticulous attention to detail are essential for the production of good picture frames. Previous experience in working with wood and an interest in furniture and restoration provided valuable assets that were put to immediate use. But there was an array of ancillary skills to be practiced and assimilated. In the section on the Craft of Framing, we outline the way in which the framer works, imparting, we hope, a flavor of the framemaker's studio. Some of the processes involved prove utterly intriguing to the layman; we will not easily forget the look of amazement on the face of our photographer when we demonstrated the application of gold leaf. At the other end of the scale come modern materials such as aluminum and plexiglass®, which provide an exciting resource for contemporary framemaking.

More intangible problems are posed when it comes to the artistic side of framemaking. Quite simply, how should you set about choosing a frame, the right frame, for your picture? The considerations that affect this choice are naturally broad and differ according to each individual. There are few if any inflexible rules to be followed, and your personal tastes and instincts are usually the best starting point. But it makes sense to approach the dilemma with a mind open to the full range of possible solutions and some knowledge of the historical background, a richly fascinating subject in its own right. Our look at the historical evolution of picture frames is not intended as an academic study; the subject is enormously complex and absorbing, combining the worlds of furniture design and art history, and is well covered by excellent specialist books. What we would like to do here is twofold. First, to provide specific historical reference points—you may be the fortunate owner of a 17th-century Italian oil painting or an early 19th-century English watercolor and want a frame, whether original or replica, as near as possible in period. But this is not the only way to benefit from a knowledge of history, and in any event few of us are lucky enough to

possess a collection of old masterpieces. An awareness of how frames evolved, both in relation to the art of the time and to lifestyles and fashion in decoration, can illuminate the way in which we make choices now, even when framing modern works. A good framer will respect historical accuracy when dealing with an old master and at the same time be prepared to borrow imaginatively from antique styles when looking at a painting executed today.

The section on Art of Framing will set out to build on the historical basis and provide an extensive guide to what can be done to enhance your picture. There are no hard and fast rules, only guidelines to help you toward a decision. There is never a single right solution—the final choice will always be influenced by a number of factors, from personal taste through to the setting in which the picture is destined to hang. But there can easily be spectacularly wrong decisions. By reading this book and referring to the wealth of illustration, you will find that you can avoid the most obvious mistakes and, making imaginative and intelligent use of all the options, arrive at the ideal solution.

Finally, we have included a section on hanging pictures. Although the serious collector of works of value may look only at the painting itself in deciding on the appropriate frame, there are many artworks, perhaps more decorative in nature, which entail other considerations. The foremost of these is the setting in which the finished piece is to hang. This is a wide subject involving interior decoration more than pure questions of framing, but it needs to be kept in mind when choices are being made.

This is not necessarily a book to be read though from start to finish, although it has been conceived so that you may do so easily and with enjoyment. Rather it is a rich mine of information, a resource to be used and returned to, allowing you to make framing choices which are confident and inspired and, above all, imaginative.

Caroline Feetham

Pias Feetham

For successful framing of original works of art, the aim above all is to provide the best possible border, enhancing the work but not competing with it. Here, a generous black frame emphasizes the strong columns of the picture, at the same time isolating it from the vivid blue background of the room.

THE
HISTORY
OF FRAMING

THE IDEA OF A FRAME OR A BORDER
DEFINING THE EDGES OF AN IMAGE AND
MARKING IT OUT FROM THE
ARCHITECTURAL SPACE AROUND IT IS A
TRADITION HISTORICALLY ASSOCIATED
WITH WESTERN ART.

Giotto's frescoes in Florence and Assisi (opposite) had borders painted around them demarcating the different scenes, containing and driving the whole narrative.

During the 18th and 19th centuries, there was a tendency to frame whole collections and genres of artwork in uniform styles of frame. This English frame from c. 1830 (left) was a conventional design for portraits of the period.

THE NEED TO CONTAIN AND SURROUND paintings already existed in Pompeii. The frescoes that adorned the walls were not only framed by the shape of the room they were in, but frequently had a border painted around them. Early Christian Byzantine mosaics had patterned borders which broadly followed the architectural lines of the church interior. When visiting a major gallery now, it is impossible to conceive of the great and often familiar paintings on display without a frame, but it would be a mistake to think that all the frames are original to, or even contemporary with, the painting. In many cases the original frames have been lost, and so galleries have had to improvise by examining those authenticated frames they do possess, or by studying some of the many paintings of 17th-century and 18th-century gallery interiors that exist.

The evolution of the picture frame ultimately relates more closely to the changing fashions and techniques in the decorative arts than in the history of art. Many collectors reframed their paintings to match interior decor and furniture. Others insisted on a uniform style of framing in order to stamp their own imprint on a collection; a form of egoism responsible for subjugating the individual qualities of a painting to the will of a patron anxious to demonstrate his wealth and power. The Comte d'Angiviller, for example, Louis XVI's superintendent of paintings, commissioned the framemaker Buteaux to design a uniform frame for the king's paintings, thereby replacing many of the original frames.

The earliest "frames" were effectively the great structures that housed the altarpieces of the 13th and 14th centuries. These were encrustations of carving and decoration, generally heavily gilded,

that mimic the façades of the great Gothic French cathedrals. At this early stage of their relationship, the artist and the maker of the altarpieces often formed part of the same workshop. As the Renaissance began to embrace the humanist ideals by which it is defined, the artist's status began to move away from that of the craftsman, and he became less concerned with the frame, or *ornamenta*. By the late 15th century, the frame was firmly in the hands of furnituremakers, woodcarvers, and even architects. But there were some artists who continued to take an interest in the design of their frames: Albrecht Dürer (1471–1528), for example, and right up to the 20th century Vincent Van Gogh (1853–90), Robert Delaunay (1885–1941), and others viewed the frame as a vital component of their work.

The Wilton Diptych (left), although representing Richard II of England, is French in origin. A small hinged altarpiece, it has two wings, hinged to allow it to be closed. The frame is made of a flat hollow ogee gilded molding. Compared to other diptychs and triptychs of the period—the 1390s—this is very simple in outline.

This altarpiece (below) also by Fra Angelico, is clearly inspired by Gothic architectural tradition.

There were many forms of tabernacle frame throughout the Renaissance, originating out of three-dimensional structures built around great altarpieces. This Italian 17th-century example (right), with an architectural pediment on Corinthian columns, combines painted details with gilded and carving. A gold design of leaves is painted on a black background.

A cassetta frame has flat moldings, as this corner detail shows (above right). It is black with gilded detailing, and a gold floral pattern runs the full length of the frame.

THE EARLY CENTURIES

The picture frame as we understand it, as an entity detached from the painting but nonetheless perceived as essential to its display and protection, emerged in the early Renaissance in Italy, and it was Italy which was to dominate the art of frame-making until the 17th century, when the center of inspiration shifted to France, just as it did in other arts.

At first, important religious paintings were housed in frames that mimicked the churches that they were to adorn—huge soaring structures essentially architectural in function and appearance. The painted panels and frame were most usually carved out of the same piece of wood, sized, gessoed, and finally painted or gilded, all in the same workshop. With the arrival of the Renaissance, along with the new philosophical and aesthetic perspective came new practices, and gradually the artist's status began to rise and the frame increasingly became the domain of craftsmen whose skills were those of the carver or engraver. As the Renaissance progressed, the interest in classical antiquity so evident in the works of the painters and architects played its part in the design of frames. There was a move away from the Gothic and toward classical forms and decorative detail.

Throughout the 15th and 16th centuries it was in Venice and Tuscany (especially Florence), in Bologna and Rome, that the most important developments in framemaking took

The aedicular frame on the Frari Altarpiece (below) by Giovanni Bellini (c. 1430–1516) was made by Jacopo da Fraenza, probably under the direction of Bellini himself, for the illusion of space within the painting is deliberately echoed in the dimensions of the structure in which it is housed, and the pilasters of the frame are taken up in the painted pilasters in the image.

place. Venetian craftsmen continued for a little longer with the traditional Gothic forms and then evolved along more flamboyant lines than their Tuscan counterparts.

Various types of frame co-existed, depending on the requirements of the painting and the pocket of the patron. Aedicular or tabernacle frames began by literally imitating temple structures, and they were very three-dimensional; in time they shed superfluous architectural aspects such as a freestanding base and retained only the pediment shape and perhaps pilasters. The circular carved frame designed to go around a circular painting was known as a tondo frame. Simple molded or plate frames known as cassetta frames were decorated with engraved, carved, or painted leaf patterns in gold, or left unadorned in black.

Sometimes gilding was combined with subtle washes of color, or simulated marble or other precious materials. Italian gilding at this early stage was generally of a lemony hue. The leaf was laid onto an ocher bole, and the whole effect was wonderfully light catching. Soft white woods and fruit woods tended to be favoured by Italian carvers.

Carved with a continuous fruit and leaf garland decoration, punctuated by the diagonal "binding" of a carved ribbon, the frame on this work by Raffaellino, dating from the early 16th century, is a very good example of a circular tondo frame (above).

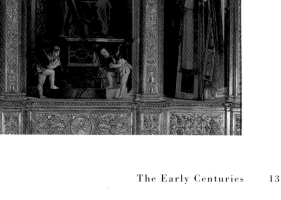

In Venice, a style of frame known as the Sansovino frame, named after the sculptor and architect Jacopo Sansovino, was to evolve during the later 16th century and into the 17th century. These frames retain certain aspects of the aedicular or tabernacle frames, such as pediments (usually broken), pilasters, and fluting, but they took the form further in an inventive and playful manner. Details such as caryatids jokingly supporting the structure were often added, along with increasingly elaborate festoons and garlands and a variety of organic shapes and spiral scrolls. These frames were either wholly gilded, or part gilded and part painted black. This emphasized the sharply graphic elements of the design.

Leaf frames, that were mainly Florentine or Bolognese in inspiration, were among the finest of the frame-carver's art in the 17th century. Large acanthus leaves were intricately intertwined and combined with open or perforated scroll work, the carver sometimes adding zoomorphic detail or a grinning grotesque face peering through the foliage. In these frames, the leaves take on a momentum of their own and flow out beyond the outer edges of the frame.

By the middle of the 17th century, what has come to be known as the Baroque gathered artists and architects, sculptors and furniture makers into its folds, sweeping across (mostly Catholic) Europe in a wave of creative energy. It was an emotional and passionate art, but attentive to the virtues of classicism. Where frame production was concerned, we find carver vying with sculptor, sometimes in a show of such virtuosity that many Baroque frames are self-sufficient superb works of art in themselves, reluctant to play second fiddle to the paintings they adorn. Many of these frames were designed to contain mirrors and form part of an interior decoration which in turn was intended to complement the outside architecture and even garden layout. The Baroque was very much an all-encompassing style.

In Northern Europe framemakers initially followed a different course. Small single-panel paintings were more common but as in Italy the earliest panel paintings were often structurally one item, the frame simply being a raised rim around the image. Later, although separate for practical purposes, the two continued to be conceived as one, and the frame largely remained the responsibility of the artist who might paint and decorate it himself, or at least direct a member of his own workshop to do so.

The small portable triptychs and diptychs (such as the Wilton Diptych) could have fairly simple frames, and straightforward moldings with plain gilding. Secular panels such as portraits, for example, might be framed simply in

The Sansovino style of frame, was current in the late 16th and early 17th centuries. It was characterized by energetic carving of scrolls and volutes, frequently including caryatids, often cherubs, as in this example (above) on a portrait of Sir Edward Hoby (1583).

In the course of the 16th century, a reaction against the classicizing influences of the Renaissance set in. In painting and sculpture, artists deliberately flouted the precepts of serenity and equilibrium inherent in classical art. They created asymmetrical compositions, unnaturally elongated and contorted figures, and introduced harsh combinations of colors, achieving through these means a very expressive but unsettling effect; this style is known as Mannerism. In the frames produced around this time, there is a move away from the restrained carving of the previous century toward a style of carving that conveys something of the neurotic restlessness and abandon found in painting and sculpture.

plain wood moldings such as oak or ebony. Later they were often veneered or painted to simulate veneer, tortoiseshell, or marble, or a variety of different stone finishes. Painting frames to resemble stone or marble extended the conceit, particularly popular in Holland, of regarding the frame around a picture as a window onto it. This would be emphasized by devising a kind of window ledge with a specially angled lower section to the frame like a window sill.

Like their Flemish neighbors, German framemakers made extensive use of plain black painted or dark natural polished woods; they made further variations by building up their wooden moldings into complicated architectural shapes; sometimes they would incorporate "outset" corners. Circular and oval paintings quite often found their place in an octagonal, heavily built-up frame, usually in polished wood. Ebonized or dark wood frames would frequently have patterning carved onto them in the so-called repeat "flame" or "wave" or "ripple" patterns; the idea being to break up the heaviness and allow light to play across the rippling.

The Sansovino-style frame (above left) is fully gilded. The extended carving and the face at the bottom give the frame a more Mannerist exaggerated feel than the more restrained silhouette of the Hoby frame (opposite).

A pierced band of profuse scrolling strapwork, rocaille, and foliate ornament decorate this Roman Baroque carved frame (left).

A late 17th-century design for a mirror by Andrea Brustolon (1662–1732) is annotated to explain the symbolism of the design: the left side is devoted to the Arts and Sciences, the right to Valor, while crowning the piece is an allegory of Love. The virtuosity of carvers enabled them to consider almost anything as worthy of their attention.

Painted flat broad frames such as this Flemish one c. 1620 (left), were frequently found in northern Europe; the imagery is usually symbolic or allegorical in nature and to the modern eye is often difficult to interpret. Another popular device was the inclusion of inscriptions on the frame, to form a part of the aesthetic of the frame as well as to inform.

This self-portrait by Dutch artist Ferdinand Bol is in a magnificent Lutma frame (below). The motifs represent sunflowers, corn cobs, and various other harvest-time plants, which are richly and ornately carved and appropriately gilded in a yellow gold.

A typically Spanish treatment of plant motifs is evident on this polychrome and gilded frame (below). The carving is robust and sculptural.

In the 17th century, a very distinct style of frame was developed in Holland, known as the Lutma frame, named after the Dutch goldsmith and engraver Jan Lutma the Younger. It is a highly ornate carved and gilded style of frame developed from the Venetian Sansovino model. Swirling and often playful motifs such as animals, fish, shells, fruit, and all kinds of plant details abound. The carvers' skills were astounding, and their apparently limitless ability to represent anything, however complex, encouraged their patrons to insist on the inclusion of more and more symbolic references such as military trophies and insignia, coats of arms, and other devices (denoting of course superior status and wealth) in preference to what might actually have been the more suitable choice of a sober black frame.

Unlike the Italian and French taste for brilliant gilding (achieved by laying gold leaf over gesso and different colored bole, or clay bases), Dutch gilding tended to be duller and more subdued, the gold leaf on occasion being applied over an oil-paint base. This method allowed the framemaker to highlight only certain areas of their carving with gold leaf and also served to keep the carved detail sharper. Even when imitating Louis XIII and Louis XIV frames, which of course many clients also wanted, the Dutch framemaker would adhere to this method of gilding.

In Spain, the earliest, most significant works were the huge retable altarpiece structures on which teams of painters, sculptors, carvers, and carpenters were employed. Apart from these great set-pieces, smaller devotional paintings tended to have frames reflecting the considerable Northern European influence already evident in Spain from the early 15th century. Such paintings would be framed in simple wood moldings, stained, polished, veneered, or painted black, as well as the wave or ripple molding frames so familiar in Germany and Holland. Later on, the black cassetta style of frame with gilded sgraffito ornament, Italian in origin, came especially to be associated with Spanish painting.

A style of frame particularly Spanish is known as the Herrera style. It takes its name from Juan de Herrera, whom Philip II of Spain commissioned to build his palace of the Escorial. This style, as applied to framemakers or other craftsmen such as *ornemanistes* and cabinetmakers, consisted of an accumulation of details applied to the basic structure, often Moorish or Gothic in origin, and often including gemstones. They were generally gilded, and frequently corner and oblong panels would be applied, along with strapwork. These frames call to mind the work on leather or gold-worked book bindings or reliquary ornaments.

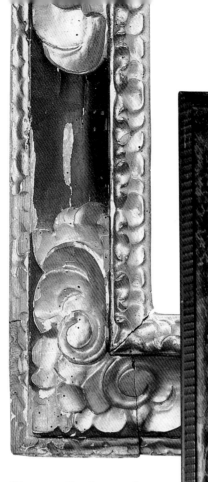

A light red tortoiseshell was used to veneer this 18th-century Dutch frame with ebony ripple and stepped outer and sight edge sections.

The center floral cartouches and carved and gilded corners on this black and gilt bolection frame (above) are characteristic of Spanish frames of the mid-17th century period.

Ripple moldings, such as these on an Alpine carved and ebonized frame (below), were designed to catch the light bouncing off the carved edges, thus breaking up an otherwise very dark area.

FRENCH INFLUENCE

Considering this portrait of the sculptor Desjardins is by Hyacinthe Rigaud (1659–1743), the principal official painter to the Court of Louis XIV, the frame is remarkably restrained.

If Italy was the dominant artistic influence in the 16th century, then it was France's turn in the 17th century. The responsibility for frame-making was to pass increasingly from painters to designers of furniture and interiors. This process had already begun in Italy and was to become even more prevalent until the advent of the 19th century. During the reign of Louis XIII, the Italian model was adopted, particularly the more restrained Bolognese style. Continuous patterns such as egg and dart or ribbon would be a feature along the inner molding, while the main body of the frame would be characterized by an undulating leaf pattern.

It was really the reign of Louis XIV at the Court of Versailles that was to set the scene for almost two centuries of French domination in the decorative arts, as in literature and architecture. French artists and craftsmen worked not only for the aristocracy at home but for foreign patrons as well, teaching and influencing local craftsmen, seeing their books of engraved illustrations disseminated far and wide and imitated by admirers right across Europe. The French authorities well understood the importance of spreading French culture and art abroad as well as satisfying the king's demands, and saw to it that excellence was encouraged; a tightly controlled network for the production of textiles and tapestries such as the Gobelins and Savonnerie works, and of porcelain such as Sèvres, was set up. Similarly, Charles le Brun, the president of that arbiter of taste, the Academy, along with other leading artists, devoted considerable time to designing frames for paintings for the royal palaces. At the same time, the guilds of craftsmen in France began to develop into centers of rigorous standards as well as being highly specialized, and among the most important were the guilds of cabinetmakers who produced all furniture made of wood, including frames for pictures and mirrors.

Stylistically, the Louis XIV frame was fairly typical of the period; deeper and finer "chiseled" carving than in the preceding period, with more stylized decoration. In the latter years of *le Roi Soleil*'s reign, the ornamentation became more substantial, with deeper carving, sharper edges, and additional decorations such as trophies (musical and military), coats of arms, heads, animals, and so forth. After Louis XIV's death in 1715, a reaction set in against the excessive Baroque splendors of Versailles and the restrictive

The Salon de L'Abondance in the palace of Versailles shows brilliantly carved and gilded frames perfectly in harmony with the magnificent decorated and gilded cornice and doorway. Note the intricately carved coats of arms and the extended corners on the frames on the far right.

way of life enjoyed by the court there. There was a move back to Paris for much of the aristocracy, who rushed to build new townhouses on a more intimate and more comfortable scale. Decorators and designers responded in a frenzy of activity with a lighter, freer style, relying on sinuous scrolling, curving lines, and asymmetrical patterns for their paneling, furniture, and frames. By the time Louis XV came of age, Rococo was in full swing and was very much a style dedicated to interior decoration, and to creating a whole look down to the smallest detail. Whereas before a certain respect had been accorded to paintings, the exuberant ornamentation on frames now became an end in itself. The sober rectangle was concealed beneath an orgy of carving and asymmetrical design in which all architectural references were banished to the advantage of frivolity over dignity. The Rococo frame exulted in itself, in its own existence; rooms were paneled into areas that "framed" paintings, windows, doors; the text on handbills was "framed" in arabesques; decorative details on furniture, porcelain, wallpaper, and textiles were frequently "framed". Vignettes proliferated. It was not until the ascension of Louis XVI that a more sober influence was felt, with a return to more classical styles.

LOUIS XIII (1610–43)

Deeply carved decoration is contained within the rectangular line of the frame. The oak used by French framemakers throughout the 18th century resulted in finer, crisper carving than the lime or poplar used in Italy.

LOUIS XIV (1643–1715)

Decoration is still largely within the frame, but carving is much finer. New motifs, including birds, different plants, shells, and palmettes, are less stylized. Ornamentation, normally with a cross-hatched background, is smaller but busier; towards the end of the period, it sometimes extends beyond the line of the frame at the corners and centers.

Louis XIII style (top left); the decoration lies within the frame.

Deeply carved foliage motifs (left) on an early Louis XIV frame.

Louis XIV baguette frame (bottom left) with crosshatched background.

This Louis XVI frame (right), with crisply carved ribbon and architecture-inspired decoration, leads the way to the simpler neoclassical style.

A fancy cartouche corner (below) is typical of Louis XV Rococo style.

The flamboyant centerpiece of a late Louis XIV-Regence frame (above), when ornamentation began to break out of the frame.

LOUIS XV (1715–74)

Stylistic changes which were beginning to occur in the early 18th century are generally grouped under the term Regence. The Rococo motifs developing at the end of the Louis XV period became more emphasized, so that cartouche scrolls at the corners and centers become more pronounced. The carved decoration seems to grow out from the linear, confines of the frame, losing its architectural origins as it takes on more flowing, fantastic, and often asymmetric forms.

LOUIS XVI (1774–92)

A reaction to the flamboyance of Rococo with a return to the straight lines of architectural and classical styles, less organic decoration, and generally less detail and cleaner lines.

A copy of an early Louis XV-style carved giltwood frame (below) shows the characteristic sinuous lines of the period.

Louis XVI baguette frame in carved giltwood, indicating a return to less flamboyant decoration (right).

An original Louis XVI mirror frame with a simple molding, showing the way to the more classical architectural lines of the later 18th century (right).

The floral decoration and arched sight edge is characteristic of Louis XV Rococo frames.

Not perhaps as flamboyant as the carving of Grinling Gibbons, this ungilded frame (right) on a portrait of Dean Swift nevertheless shows the typical elements of a mid-17th century portrait frame of its kind. It bears numerous references to the qualities and character of the sitter, which allow the carver to give full rein to his skills.

The carved room in Petworth House in Sussex (below) bears testimony to the extraordinary virtuosity of Grinling Gibbons in the limewood carvings that surround and embrace the paintings.

BRITISH DEVELOPMENTS

During the 17th century, Britain produced some interesting variants of the styles being developed on the continent. Until then English frames were basically flat, painted black with an oblique gilded inner edge, perhaps with Italian-style decoration or ornamentation applied at the corners and in the center of each length. The reign of Charles I, which saw an openness to foreign influence in the visual arts and an enormous growth in patronage, both royal and aristocratic, ushered in a taste for elaborate gilded frames. Many of these were openly Italianate in inspiration, based on the Venetian Sansovino model, but equally important were the frames executed in the auricular style, characterized by organic motifs punctuated at the top and bottom by masklike centerpieces based on lion's heads or grotesque human faces.

As the century progressed, with its various political and artistic upheavals, the pendulum swung between French and Dutch stylistic influences, particularly after the ascension of William of Orange to the throne. The Sunderland frame (named after the Duke of Sunderland because of his prediliction for framing many of his pictures in this style of frame) owes much both to the earlier auricular styles and to the contemporary Lutma frames of Holland, with broad Baroque swept carving. The Lely frame, named after the artist Sir Peter Lely (1618–80), was a sort of "institutional" frame devised for King Charles II's gallery at Windsor.

However, the triumph of English 17th frame-making can be found in the work of the virtuoso woodcarver Grinling Gibbons (1648-1721). He, too, had Dutch connections, having been born in Rotterdam, but he was in fact English, returning to England in 1672. He was introduced to Charles II, became Master Carver in Wood to the Crown, and worked on numerous large projects. He worked for Sir Christopher Wren at Hampton Court Palace, carving cornices, door-surrounds, and overmantels, and he also created a number of brilliantly exuberant frames, made up of what seemed to be entirely three-dimensional garlands of fruit, leaves, and flowers springing from a wide flat inner molding.

In the early 18th century, it was principally the French style that influenced frame-making in Britain, as in so much of Europe. Although some well-known figures, such as the architect William Kent (1685–1748), produced designs, it was French Regence and Louis XV Rococo that were to

dominate. As in France, the use of the frame within the overall interior decor was in its heyday; pictures and frames, paneling, and furniture were conceived as a whole.

A particular interest in Chinese subjects led the cabinet-maker and designer Thomas Chippendale (1718–79) to imitate bamboo, stylized bird cages, and rock arrangements for his carvings and to create picture frames that were fantastical and lightly spun creations. In his work one can trace the evolution from his own particular form of Rococo to the stirrings of neoclassical sobriety that was to come as welcome relief from the candyfloss frivolities of the mid-18th century. His 1754 publication *Gentleman and Cabinet Makers Director* illustrated a full range of furniture with exotic motifs and sinuous curves. But by the 3rd Edition in 1762, there were distinct shifts toward a more restrained approach, heralding the influence of neoclassicism.

The phenomenon of the Grand Tour and renewed interest in classical antiquity led many young Englishmen to visit Rome; one of these visitors was the young Robert Adam (1728–92), who on his return to England applied all that he had seen to his architecture and interior design. This return to relative sobriety led Sir Joshua Reynolds (1723–92) and other fashionable artists to favor the classical Carlo Maratta style of frame, although if their clients preferred they would also use a simplified Rococo frame. Both styles fit happily into an English late 18th-century decorative scheme.

One of the most perfect of Robert Adam's interiors can be found at Kedleston Hall, Derbyshire (above left). He selected frames to complement the decoration and furniture—in a sense, the paintings themselves were ancillary to the interior design. Mantelpieces, tables, mirrors, and paintings were placed together as an entity.

Originally this mid-17th century frame (above right) would have been gessoed and gilded. The process of cleaning off black paint, probably applied at the end of the 19th century as a mark of respect for a death, revealed the delicate carving.

This portrait of the Earl and Countess of Essex is contained in an auricular Sunderland frame, gilded over solid Baroque carving, in fine contrast to the Adam frame of 100 years later.

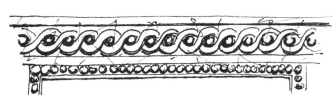

Guilloche patterns are made up of interlocking spirals that form a continuous band. Originating in Italy, they were very popular in 18th-century British ornamentation.

RESTORATION (1660–85)

His exile having been spent in France and Holland, on his restoration to the British throne in 1660 Charles II brought a taste for continental fashion. Baroque motifs, trophies, cherubs, and virtuoso carving—all appear in the work of Grinling Gibbons, perhaps the archetypal exponent of these influences. Both Lely and Kneller frames are contemporary with Gibbons but represent a separate, restrained ornamentation.

PALLADIANISM

A style inspired by the architecture of Andrea Palladio (1508–80). In his publications he codified the classical

A Kent frame (left), with sand-gritted center and carved rosettes at the top corners.

A carved Lely panel frame (top right): the burnished panels punctuate the carved foliate decoration around the length of the frame.

Outline of the 1733 Kent frame devised and carved for the Kit Kat Club portraits by Sir Godfrey Kneller (1649–1723).

A carved giltwood frame in Chippendale style with the familiar Rococo sinuous lines (center right).

This variation on a Lely frame (left) is carved gilt wood with a hazed background.

The standard neo-classical frame favored by English portrait painters (right), known as the Carlo Maratta or Salvatore Rosa style.

Roman and Renaissance stylistic precedents that were so popular. Knowledge of his work was brought to Britain by Inigo Jones (1573–1652) in the early 17th century. Originally an architectural style, it was revived in the early 18th century by Lord Burlington, to embrace interior decoration and furnishing style as well. William Kent was a protegé of Lord Burlington, and is the best known of the architects and designers working in this manner.

CHIPPENDALE

Thomas Chippendale was a household name. His stylistic evolution is significant because it both led and encapsulated the developments that were taking place in Britain from the Rococo style, including the neogothic and chinoiserie elements of the 1740s and 50s to the neoclassical style as introduced by Robert Adam in the late 1760s.

A late 17th-century carved giltwood frame (top left).

A carved giltwood Kneller frame with a fleur-de-lis at the top and oak leaf decoration (top center).

A gilt oval frame with a discreet running carved decoration (far right). It would most likely have been used for a portrait.

A Kent frame (right) dating to the mid 18th century, showing the outset corner design.

The Hogarth frame (above) commonly combined a black outer frame with a gilded inner section, most often used for prints.

The frame on this French-School painting of a lady sitting in her parlor is typically neoclassical: clean, uncluttered lines, simple detailing on the sight edge, and to give it more importance and focus, an elaborate decorative bow carved to sit on top.

Elegant veneered and gilded Louis XVI furniture and family portraits of the same period all complement one another in the salon of the Chateau de Canon in Normandy, France (below).

NEOCLASSICISM, EMPIRE, REGENCY

In the visual and decorative arts, the movement that began to take hold after the excesses of the Baroque and the sinuous intricacies of the Rococo is known as neoclassicism. It originated in Rome in the mid-18th century, largely driven by the discovery in 1748 of the ruins of Herculaneum and Pompeii, and then spread rapidly through the rest of Europe as an inspiration to artists and craftsmen of all kinds. Thus in frames as in the other decorative arts, classically inspired details began to return, without the fantastic elaborations of previous generations, but with a genuine attempt at authenticity fueled by the new archeological discoveries. There is no one style that represents the neoclassical frame as such, but rather a number of styles that adopt one or other classicizing detail, by and large building on a comparatively crisp and clean outline. For example, simple guilloche fretwork patterning running the length of the molding; scoop profiles with ribbon or reeded outer edges; continuous laurel-leaf patterning; details such as simple rosettes set at the corners; fluting: all were used at this time. Straight moldings might be surmounted with an arrangement of elements such as a vase, a wreath, or an intertwining composition of birds and animals all held together with garlands and ribbons which sometimes hang down the sides.

After these essentially decorative borrowings, neo-classicism gradually began to pay more attention to form and shape, resulting in a simpler outline. This was particularly so with furniture, but it also applied to frames, though perhaps in a less immediately obvious way, since gilding continued to play a prominent part in frame decoration, somewhat obfuscating the more architectural lines and simpler (though still classically inspired) ornamentation. This new formalism was most evident in frames which made use of woods and wood veneers with appliquéd or inlaid decoration.

French Empire style, although chronologically only spanning the period of Napoleon's reign as Emperor, sprang from and continued into what one might dub mature neo-classicism. Egyptian decorative motifs and forms were now added to the major influence of ancient Greece, due largely to the inspiration derived by artists and designers from Napoleon's Egyptian expedition, in particular from the famous *Voyage dans la Basse et Haute-Egypte* published in Paris and London in 1802 by the archeologist and engraver Vivant

Denon. It was his designs that were to become the major inspiration for what is known as Empire style, recognizable by its use of decorative devices such as the lotus leaf, the palm, the chimera, sphinxes, and many other oriental symbols and imagery.

Although inevitably affected by the Egyptian frenzy from across the Channel, and by French taste and French craftsmen that had migrated across in the preceding revolutionary period, the English style remains quite distinct – what is now referred to as Regency. As Chippendale had done before him, Thomas Sheraton (1751–1806) produced a cabinet dictionary in which he summed up many of the newer tendencies that made up the Regency style. With the publication of his *Cabinet Maker, Upholsterer and General Artist's Encyclopedia*, issued in several parts between 1804 and 1806, he was one of the first to illustrate the Egyptian themes which were to inspire artists and designers.

A portrait by Frans Van der Mijn (1719–83) who had close connections with England (above); though the picture was painted in 1750 the frame is late 18th century.

This corner detail of the Mijn portrait (above right) shows how the earlier bravado has given way to a much more elegant and restrained approach to framing, particularly on paintings on a domestic scale.

The carved and gilded oval frame (above) is original to this British School portrait of a sitter in naval uniform, painted c. 1770.

An Empire-style frame surrounds a French provincial mid-19th century portrait of a boy. By the early to mid-19th century, frames made from plaster or composition were being made in earlier styles.

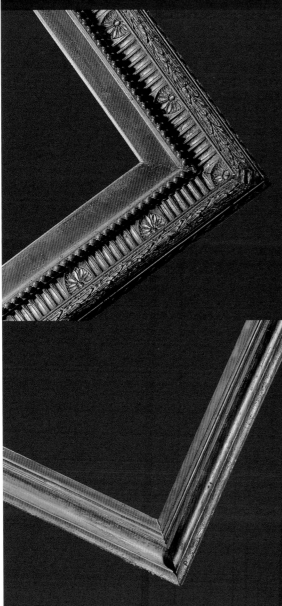

NEOCLASSICISM (*C.* 1770–1830)

In the second half of the 18th century, artists and architects across northern Europe began to reject the highly ornate Rococo style and turned to the purer lines and classical decoration inspired by the new wave of interest in classical antiquity. Frames became more architectural and linear, and if decorated they were given finely carved floral designs, ribbons, and fluting. As they were now lighter and less imposing, in order to draw attention to a particularly important sitter, in the case of a portrait, they were often given carved decorations, usually of classical derivation, at the top of the frame.

Oval carved Regency frame (top left), with gadrooned top edge and beaded shot sight edge.

Anthemia and rosette decoration on Empire hollow frames (above).

Regency frame with lamb's tongue design on the sight edge (right).

A hollow profile Regency frame (center left), decorated with a fluted band interspersed with rosette motifs, and a ribbon twist design.

A simple Regency gilt hollow frame (left).

French late neoclassical urn decoration carved at the top of an otherwise simple frame

EMPIRE (1804–14)

In France the neoclassical tendency hardened into severity during the revolutionary period and just after, finally emerging into the Empire style which was to be imitated across Europe. It retained a simple linear outline and many of the more basic classical motifs, with the addition of Egyptian motifs.

REGENCY (1811–20)

The English equivalent to Directoire and Empire styles, Regency had its roots in late neoclassicism. It embraced Greek, Roman, Rococo, Gothic, and Egyptian elements and motifs.

A Louis XVI ribbon-top frame (center top) with laurel leaf and berry garland against a fluted background.

A return to architectural lines defines this Louis XVI frame (left): the ornamentation is restricted to the top.

English Regency gilt hollow frame with running laurel leaf design and beaded top edge (above right).

Regency gilt hollow frame with shot and stick pattern along the sight edge (right).

AMERICAN NATIVE STYLES

In early colonial days, the settlers were rarely wealthy, and such paintings as they possessed were generally very simply framed, often using window or door-trim moldings painted black. Gradually, with the growth of towns and cities came a more affluent way of life, and with that came luxuries such as paintings and fine furniture.

From about the mid-18th century, the development of the frame in America follows two paths. The first broadly echoes the current styles in Europe, initially through the examples of directly imported items of furniture and frames, and through the indispensable pattern books from England and France which could be studied and copied, fairly crudely at first, but with increasing skill as local craftsmen gained experience. By the late 18th century, framemakers began to be established as fine craftsmen in their own right. Portrait frames in particular were frequently made by craftsmen, known as mirror-makers, who were also responsible for the intricate carvings for furniture. During the course of this

The Fraktur room in the Winterthur Museum, Delaware (above), shows a selection of old American pictures in an appropriately decorated setting. Stencil work and vinegar painting give an impression of simplicity and humility.

A common practice of early American framers was to make frames from window moldings, possibly the origin of this simple black frame. It is quite substantial in relation to the picture it contains.

evolution, they learned to modify and adapt the European styles to suit the more sober tastes of the American people (reflecting perhaps their largely Protestant ancestry at the time), and to enjoy the superb carving qualities and durability of the indigenous white pine from which most frames were made at that period.

Some names of American framemakers are known to us, such as James Reynolds from Philadelphia who was a fine carver and gilder working in the latter part of the 18th century, and Charles Robinson, also of Philadelphia, who worked at the beginning of the 19th century. Certain painters—John Singleton Copley (1738–1815), for example —positively favored the most fashionable European styles of the day, in his case a particular type of intricately carved and gilded Rococo frame with open carved corners and center points with floral crests. John Wollaston, a prolific colonial painter in the middle of the 18th century, has also come to be associated with a particular type of European-inspired frame: delicate and lacy with open corners and center panels, with a crosshatched background pattern.

Coexisting with the stylish Philadelphian and Charleston framemakers, whose sophisticated clients required them to look to Europe for inspiration, other framemakers were

involved in making what is perhaps the most significant and recognizably North American contribution to the art of the frame. Frames with simple flat moldings in black painted pine, or unadorned natural indigenous woods such as maple or fruitwoods, or painted to imitate veneer, seem to spring most directly from those earliest colonial days and owe nothing to the prevailing European fashions.

Sometimes the framemakers, taking their cue from the painting, would introduce idiosyncratic stenciled or carved details; sometimes they would adapt typical architectural details to be found on many mid-18th century American doorways and mantelpieces, like the so-called crosseted-corner style, frequently used to frame embroidered works.

The names of many of the styles are associated with their designers or with the artists who used them for their paintings: thus the Sully style, named after the artist Thomas Sully (1783–1872), usually refers to a broad gilded frame with a simple sloped profile and a raised outer rim, often containing within it a broad gilded insert, with a circular or oval opening for a miniature portrait. The Hicks frame, commonly used around 1820 to 1850, popularized by the artist Edward Hicks (1780–1849), uses corner blocks and sometimes stencil decoration similar to that painted on

This charming pair of watercolors of Mr. and Mrs. Lott (above), painted in 1819, are imaginatively framed in birds'-eye maple veneered flat frames, with cutout fishtail designs at the top and an inlaid heart. Made from readily available and comparatively inexpensive materials, these frames show the originality of the American craftsman.

A simple molding, gilded over red bole, frames this early 19th-century primitive American portrait of a little girl (right).

An intricate grapevine border frames this view of Eagle Mills, New York (right), possibly painted by the American artist Thomas Wilson (c. 1811–77). Wilson was also a carriage painter, and the decoration indicates the work of a skilled craftsman. It bears testimony to the American fascination for decoration, whether stenciled or freestyle.

The simple yet elegant frame on this 19th-century watercolor (left) shows the inventiveness of framemakers faced with a limited choice of mouldings. The figured veneer is edged with gilt, the identical molding being reversed to form the narrow outer band.

Edward Hicks was a painter and a skilled sign, coach, and decorative painter. As in the frames around these paintings (above), he frequently employed inscriptions as part of his frame, and on this one he also used corner blocks, a favorite device of his.

furniture. A familiar style is that of the Limner frame, used on many portraits painted in rural America between 1750 and 1850. This is a variant on the flat, totally unadorned black frame, having a scoop-shaped profile painted black with a gilded outer and inner rim. Just as American naïve painting has its own unique identity, so does the framing that went with it, and these styles represent the benchmark by which modern framers will consider framing primitive paintings, embroidery, and prints, as well as modern works.

In the later years of the 19th century, one of the most significant influences on the evolution of frame-making in Britain and Europe came from the American painter James Abbott McNeill Whistler (1834–1903). He regarded his frames and paintings as part of a larger aesthetic concept that included the entire room and its furnishings. As he said to the collector George A. Lucas: "You will notice that I have designed my frames as carefully as my pictures—and thus they form as important a part as any of the rest of the work—carrying on the particular harmony throughout." In this he was reflecting the many *Fin de Siécle* movements that were evolving, which sought to marry the different elements of interior decoration, many of them stylistically owing much to the 19th-century passion for all things Japanese.

Broadly speaking, he developed three styles of frame for his work. The first had a flat profile decorated with low-relief abstracted Chinese or Japanese ornament and pattern. The second, made up of delicately reeded moldings, had the Japanese motifs painted on with colors that harmonized with the colors of the painting. The third had an inward sloping, quite substantial reeded-trim frame. It is interesting to note that Whistler's frames were made by the same framemakers who worked for Pre-Raphaelite painters William Holman Hunt (1827–1910) and Dante Gabriel Rossetti (1828–82). Like Rossetti, he frequently made use of the dot and arrow motif against the picture. Just as his "butterfly" trademark appeared on his paintings, so it appeared in 1871 for the first time painted in red on the left side of the frame for his painting *Variations in violet and green*. Another decorative motif of which he was particularly fond was the stylized fish scale or wave pattern, which can be seen on the frame for the famous *Old Battersea Bridge*.

Stanford White (1853–1901) was an architect and designer mixing with the rich and powerful in American society. His frames consisted of subtle accretions of classical architectural detail with strong forms. His frames achieved enough recognition to be patented and reproduced after his death by the Newcomb-Macklin Company.

In contrast to the unworldliness of a Hicks frame or the simple elegance of a plain maple frame, the decoration in this room (above) in Mount Vernon, Virginia, shows the prevailing European neo-classical style as it transferred to the wealthy and sophisticated in the America of the 1820s. The light-painted paneled wood provided an elegant backdrop for displaying works of art.

Whistler's painting Variations in violet and green *(left) is framed in an excellent example of one of the frames designed with such care and attention by the artist himself for his own work. His famous butterfly signature appears on the top left of the frame.*

A portrait of the composer Robert Schumann, painted by J. F. Klima in 1839 (left), is soberly framed in veneered wood with a lighter wood inlay at the sight edge and outer edge. Different colored inlaid woods were used to vary the emphasis of a frame—a technique that increased in popularity in the course of the 19th century.

These engravings illustrating the story of William Tell (above) are in original Swedish Biedermeier print frames, typically made in birchwood with applied ebony corners and brass rosettes. This was a very satisfactory way to frame prints, and there are many variations of this simple formula.

A standard mid-19th century highly decorated plaster composition gilt frame has been used for this portrait (below) by a follower of Frans Xaver Winterhalter (1803–73). Although the opening is oval, the painting itself is rectangular in shape—this was a standard framing practice.

GERMANY AND SCANDINAVIA

In Germany and Bavaria, neoclassical influence continued well into the later 1820s and even 1830s. In Berlin, the classical architect Friedrich Schinkel (1781–1841) exerted a great deal of influence, not only in his architecture, but also through his designs for interiors of royal palaces and public buildings. His was essentially an aristocratic Prussian neoclassical style, less zealously antiquarian in the accuracy of his classical references than his British or French peers. He was responsible for the development of the Schinkel frame, characterized by a relatively simple concave molding rising up from the painting, with palmette patterns along the length and leaf decoration at the corners.

The Empire and Regency styles were to have more influence on southern Germany. With the increasing demand for simpler, more practical furniture from the emerging middle classes, the severe contours of the Empire style evolved into a more intimate bourgeois style which was known as Biedermeier. The emphasis was on simplicity: less bronze or gilt extraneous decoration, and greater use of natural polished woods, particularly the lighter indigenous fruit woods, sometimes with outlines or decorations created by ebony or ebonized fruit wood inlays. The telltale neoclassical and Empire motifs reappear on frames in the form of inlays and marquetry. Scandinavia, too, was influenced by Empire style both in its aristocratic, or rather Napoleonic, form (particularly in Sweden, in the grand furniture, decoration and frames of its palaces), and in a variation not unlike Biedermeier style, popular in Denmark. During the Napoleonic Wars, the Swedes remained sympathetic to France; they even invited one of Napoleon's marshals to become crown prince, thus establishing the Bernadotte dynasty. This close relationship no doubt accounts for the almost pure French Empire style found in Sweden.

During the wars however, mahogany became difficult to obtain, so the Scandinavians, like the Germans, made use of their own much lighter native woods: alder, maple, ash, and birch, which frequently stood in for satinwood. Frames made out of these woods could then be decorated with marquetry or inlay in darker woods. This decoration at first acted as a substitute for the gilt bronze or gilt ornamentation so typical of French Empire, but has long become admired as a form of ornamentation in its own right.

Stocklosters House, near Stockholm, was built for Great Commander Gustav Wrangel in the mid-17th century. The frames and the interior of the great hall (above) reflect the French influence in aesthetic matters that was very strong among the Swedish aristocracy, while the painted work on the door and dado owe a lot to the rich native folk inheritance.

Here the walls, decorated in a mixture of freestyle and stenciled vinegar painting, give an idiosyncratic, richly patterned background for the oval gilt frame above the door in this interior in Gripsholm Castle in Sweden (right). A more typically indigenous Scandinavian style of frame is the unadorned fruitwood frame glimpsed at the right-hand edge of the picture, which fits comfortably with this decoration.

THE 19TH CENTURY

From an aesthetic point of view, there is very little to distinguish the general run of middle and later 19th-century frames in Europe and North America, with the exception of the much more sympathetic treatment devised for American primitive painting. The development of mass-production methods in the 19th century, such as molded plaster-cast ornament, accelerated the decline of finely carved original work and opened the way to a remarkably eclectic approach to frame-making. This was a period of rapidly increasing affluence. Painters were now painting for the middle classes, aided by the new breed of professional dealers who were in turn encouraging this growing market. To satisfy the demand from a relatively conservative clientele, framemakers responded by producing inferior copies of previous styles, such as Louis XIII and XIV or the so-called Barbizon frame which was often used for landscape paintings, its wide, substantial character lending such paintings a comforting air of importance. One of the ways of persuading a hesitant purchaser, whose confidence in their own taste might be a little shaky was to "package" the work in such a way that it would both feel familiar and sit comfortably in an average bourgeois interior. If it was heavily gilded, it would also indicate a satisfying degree of wealth.

At the same time, the increase in museums of art and collections that were open to the public resulted in a greater demand for standard styles of frame that would unify the works, a trend that developed in the late 18th century. Under Napoleon, for example, nearly every painting in the Louvre had been put into Empire frames; a choice entirely in tune for a painting by David, but wholly inappropriate on something painted a century earlier. Composition plaster frames were ideal for mass framing of this sort since they were cheap and quick to produce.

Inevitably there was to be a reaction. In England, this first found expression in the Arts and Crafts Movement and in the philosophy of its founder, the socialist writer and designer William Morris (1834–96). His revulsion against industrialism and the decline of the craftsman led him to promote a revival in medieval standards of craftsmanship, allied to the concept of designing for the living environment as a whole, with applied and fine arts as equal partners in the objective of designing everything for the home, from

Built in the late 19th century for Theodore Mander, Wightwick Manor, near Wolverhampton, is a tribute to John Ruskin and William Morris. Note the Morris wallpaper, the Pre-Raphaelite portrait, and the drawing in a simple reeded frame with corner blocks.

Rossetti designed the frame for Beata Beatrix *(left), with its neoplatonic symbols in the medallions and inscription incorporated into the frame, intended to expand on the theme of the painting. Emblems of this kind were a frequently used device of the Pre-Raphaelites.*

Highly gilded and burnished aedicular frames recall the portals of Greek temples. The frame is brought into play as an element of the illusion of space created within the painting. Lord Leighton particularly favored this style of frame, though each one was carefully designed to go with a particular painting, as here for The Bracelet.

Evening Sunset, by a follower of Thomas Hand (below), is in a typical frame of the period, designed to appeal to the new middle classes. It has an 18th-century look, but is a 19th-century mass-produced composition plaster frame.

May Morning on Magdalen Tower (right) perfectly encapsulates all that Pre-Raphaelite framing sought to achieve: design and material harmonize to create an entirely successful unity.

This frame (below) combines characteristic Pre-Raphaelite elements; reeding with rosette detail, a flat inner section, and a running leaf pattern.

The originality of the frame on Franz von Stuck's Die Sünde, *or* The Sin *(above), lies in the conjunction of the classical references in the aedicular frame imitating a Greek temple with the modern disks and inscription panel at the base.*

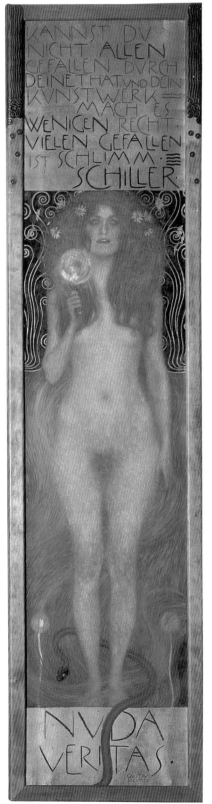

Design, inscription, and painting all form an integral design-conscious entity for Gustav Klimt's 1899 work Nuda Veritas. *The top and bottom panels of the picture seem to cross over into the realm of the frame, while the frame itself, with its applied metal corners, consists of a deceptively simple flat molding.*

architecture, furniture, wallpaper, and textiles to dishes and flatware. Greatly influenced by Morris, and fellow founders of his movement, were the Pre-Raphaelite painters Ford Madox Brown (1821–96), Edward Burne-Jones (1833–98), Rossetti, and Holman Hunt. In their attitude to framing, as in their painting, they too looked to the early Italian and Flemish masters for inspiration. They devised and oversaw the construction of frames specifically intended to match and complement their paintings, insisting on a return to properly carved, gessoed and gilded frames. In design, many of these were based on early Italian models such as the tabernacle or aedicular frame especially favored by Burne-Jones, Lord Frederic Leighton (1830–96) and Lawrence Alma-Tadema (1836–1912). In the earlier years of the Pre-Raphaelite brotherhood, both painting and frame were often didactic or religious in approach. Further emphasizing their debt to the early masters, and of course in line with their didactic purpose, inscriptions, sometimes quite extensive, would form a part of the design of the frame.

A very late frame designed by Holman Hunt for his painting *May Morning on Magdalen Tower* (illustrated on page 37) was executed in beaten copper, a material favored by the Pre-Raphaelites. Hunt was so proud of this particular work that he wished he could have shown it to the art critic John

Ruskin (1819–1900): "I feel sure that he would have been much pleased with it, and even be encouraged to hope better for the artistic life of our country by seeing it."

Particularly associated with Rossetti and Ford Madox Brown is a design known as the reed and roundel type of frame. Variations of this have an outer frame that is reeded and ornamented with low-relief round bosses and perhaps squares, a central simple sloping section gilded directly onto the untreated wood (usually oak) rather than on a bole base, thereby showing the grain. Rossetti called them "ornaments of the chess square or wheel kind". More complicated developments of this type of frame involved further embellishments to the roundel, or replacing the reeded exterior and interior mouldings with reed and ribbon or bead and reel type patterns (known as astragal or baguette). The carved and etched details usually contained in roundels would frequently underline the "message" of the painting through supportive symbols.

The same distaste for mass production was mirrored across Europe, with a great many artists taking framing matters into their own hands, looking to the Renaissance for inspiration. The Symbolist painter Gustave Moreau (1826–98) did so in France with his extensive use of tabernacle frames, as did Franz von Lenbach (1836–1904) in Germany. Many of Lenbach's paintings were virtually pastiches in Renaissance style, and the frames designed to complement this. He produced Sansovino frames, as well as many familiar examples of Renaissance carving, lavishly gilded, with frequent classical references; they were well adapted to High Victorian taste and were well accepted by clients. Sketches of his also testify to his concern for envisaging painting, frame, and wall space as a single unified ensemble.

By the end of the 19th century, alongside the advances in painting being made by the Impressionists and the neo-Impressionists, various artists that we recognize as belonging to a quite different aesthetic—that of Art Nouveau—began to

form into groups and associations, all of them espousing ideas that had their roots in the English Arts and Crafts movement. An intense interest in the frame and in its place, both around the pictures and in the context of interior decoration, as well as the many stylistic indicators, mark this comparatively brief but very distinctive period.

Franz von Stuck (1863–1928) in Munich and Gustav Klimt (1862–1918) in Vienna were leading artists of their generation and of their respective Secession movements, and were among the first to have been trained in design as well as in the fine arts. Like their Arts and Crafts predecessors they were eager to break down the barriers between art and craft. Both artists created frames that were consciously designed to integrate the paintings with their environment where applicable, as well as to complement the works of art themselves, in some cases creating frames that were integral to the balance and design of the painting itself.

Fernand Knopff (1858–1921) in Brussels, a member of the *Fin de Siècle* group of artists Les XX, was greatly influenced not only by the Arts and Crafts movement, but also by Whistler and by Japanese sources, favoring broad flat wooden moldings with punched or embossed decoration, sometimes metal, sometimes leather. Frequently his frames take on the dual role of frame and mat.

Jan Toorop (1858–1928), a Dutch Symbolist painter, was like so many artists at this time greatly influenced by Japanese examples, and in the most characteristic of his works the frame and the painting are so firmly linked that, to an extent, the balance of the one makes no sense without the other. In order to achieve this, he tended to use very flat broad frames onto which he would continue the imagery of the painting.

After his departure from the Secession in 1905, Klimt began to use more minimal framing, preferring to treat his paintings as murals that needed just a simple band. In this he was perhaps presaging a time when artists would seek to reject the need for a frame altogether.

Continuous wavy lines are characteristic of Jugenstil design, and for his Portrait of a Lady *(below left), Klimt has used them to decorate the flat sloping central panel of his frame. The outer and inner carved moldings serve both to contain the central section and to echo details in the portrait such as the woman's necklace.*

This gilded frame, in origin 17th-century Spanish (right), has been transformed by the addition of late 19th-century Art Nouveau decoration with a sinuous, twining floral motif.

THE IMPRESSIONISTS

The Impressionists, unlike Whistler and the later Secession artists, did not see their paintings and frames as part of a whole interior design and had no quarrel with the notion of a frame as a demarcation or a boundary around the edges of their pictures. But they did take a keen interest in the presentation of their works in the context of the exhibitions they put on in defiance of the "official" outlets provided by the Establishment. They did not care for the systematic mid-19th century use of over-elaborate gilded composition frames such as they saw surrounding otherwise "modern" paintings exhibited in the salon exhibitions.

As a result, several of them began to devise other ways of framing their works. Edgar Degas (1834–1917) and Camille Pissarro (1830–1903) were particularly active in working out new profiles and approaches, and both were quite sensitive to changes made in their own framing decisions by dealers and buyers. Degas was known to have pursued collectors who had had the temerity to replace his frames with new ones! His notebooks are full of sketches for frame designs, and Pissarro's letters contain frequent references to colors and other frame details concerning his pictures. Several options and compromises were worked out, and although in many cases these are now lost to posterity the various references to them still provide a good guide as to how the artists felt their works should be displayed.

The frame most closely associated with the Impressionists is what the critic Felix Feneon defined in 1886 as the "classic white Impressionist frame", which at the time symbolized modernity. In fact it was a carved Louis XV or Louis XVI frame denuded of its gilding and then painted white, or occasionally a color. The use of white as a framing color was an important innovation, and Degas particularly liked it for his paintings. In part, this came about as a result of the artists' following the color theories of Chevreuil; the idea being that white would best reflect and intensify the colors found in the paintings. He felt the neutrality of white to be very satisfying. Later, Degas and Pissarro would modify the white toward shades of gray, a move also approved by Chevreuil. Apart from the stripped-back carved frames, the modern compromise that both the artists and their dealer Paul Durand-Ruel found they could agree upon was a frame with a fluted outer molding, usually painted white, or

sometimes gilded and burnished. Pierre August Renoir (1841–1919) was probably the Impressionist artist most at ease with a standard mid-19th century Louis XVI-style frame in its gilded state, and it is true that the warmth of his colors and the touch of his brush sit well in the more opulent gilded frames.

Although the least successful of the Impressionists in his life time, another artist for whom the frames were of paramount importance was Vincent Van Gogh. He, too, tried to reconcile the color theories that were around at the time with suggestions to his brother and agent Theo. Like Georges Seurat (1859–91), he took to painting borders around his later paintings, often in bright red; it seems that he, too, favored white for the frames.

Impressionist oil paintings are frequently found under glass; this is because they preferred not to use varnish which is prone to yellow over time and thus radically alter the freshness and the relative value of the colors.

The frame on Degas's Apres le bain, femme s'essuyant la nuque is ribbed rather than grooved, and gilded with a flat gold finish. This type of frame was frequently used by Degas, and he varied the finish depending on the colors in his paintings.

Seurat's theories about color led him to his pointilliste technique, which he extended to borders around his works and onto the frames. The outer frame on The Circus (above right) is flat with four grooved channels, lightly gilded on a white bole.

A standard Louis XV copy, favored by dealers for Impressionist paintings, has been used here for Pissarro's Soleil couchant à Eragny. The pale white gold has been knocked back to provide softer frame tones.

A corner of a stripped carved frame (right) shows the sort of look that was popular with Impressionists and their dealers. The residue of gesso and red bole can be seen in the deeper areas. Sometimes a frame like this would be painted white or washed over in color.

MASS PRODUCTION

The 19th century saw the industrialization of frame making, as of many other activities that had previously been undertaken by specialized craftsmen. The development of plaster composition or "compo" moldings made it possible to reproduce any style or ornamentation from preceding periods. Numerous adaptations were made for the home, including a huge variety of narrower designs intended for the burgeoning market of watercolors and drawings, that were increasingly being bought for display as works of art in their own right.

Swept frames (above left), composition copies of earlier styles.

Two English watercolor frames (top left), one wedge profile, one with cross ribbon decoration.

Late 19th-century French arch-topped frame with a running floral pattern (left).

Whistler-inspired frame (above) with embossed patterning on the flat panel and reeding on the outer section.

Victorian watercolor frames (below), with raised corner decorations of ferns, thistles, flowers, and leaves.

Typical Pre-Raphaelite combination of reeding interrupted by roundels and corner blocks, the flat area gilded so the grain shows through.

German frame showing the strong Gothicizing tendency, also found in American frames.

French papier-mâché frame (below) with scrolls and flowers on a cross-hatched background.

A simple Florentine cassetta style design (bottom center), known as a Watts frame.

A simple English leaf decoration on a hollow frame (bottom right).

Typical 19th-century molded plaster applied plamette decoration.

An oval-spandrel frame with corner decorations of lyres and masks (right).

Late 19th-century French rounded corner frame (below right) with raised "D" profile .

ARTS AND CRAFTS

The Arts and Crafts movement spearheaded the reaction against mass-production copies of earlier patterns. Artists, inspired by the example and teachings of William Morris, demanded frames made to their own specifications and designs. They sought a return to traditional materials, to skilled carving, and to gilding. Some took the early Renaissance model as their inspiration, while others such as Whistler made up new designs which proclaimed an entirely new departure for the framing of contemporary work.

THE 20TH CENTURY

In the visual arts generally, conventional notions have been blown apart, and this extends to notions of framing. There is potential for an unprecedented conflict of interest between artist, dealer, museum and private collector. During the 19th century, artists had already begun to exert a great deal of influence over the presentation of their paintings, and some artists were integrating their frames to such an extent that it was impossible for paintings to be detached from their frames without altering the balance and design of the painting itself. At the opposite end of the spectrum, artists like Kasimir Malevich (1878–1935) and Piet Mondrian (1872-1944) rejected frames altogether, a preference that is still displayed by many abstract artists, particularly the American Abstract Expressionists, as part of the ethos of their work. They allow shapes and colors to enter into the living space around them, in some sense to become one with the surrounding area.

An important development started by the Impressionists and the neo-Impressionists has been continually explored and returned to again and again in the 20th century—that of the frame painted as if to continue the painting out beyond its natural boundaries. French artist Robert Delaunay explored this idea as part of his concern with color and movement. In England, working rather more recently, Howard Hodgkin does a similar thing in his paintings.

Pablo Picasso (1881–1973) and Georges Braque (1882–1963) both had old and antique frames in their studios, but Daniel Kahnweiler, their dealer, preferred to frame their Cubist paintings in plain black moldings lying flush with the picture. It seems that Braque's own preference during this period was for reverse moldings. He felt these helped to project the fragmented imagery toward the viewer and away from the picture plane, simultaneously creating a slightly ambiguous sculptural aspect to his work.

The crisp white edges of frames generally selected for the paintings of Piet Mondrian not only complement the paintings, but also suggest a modernity and geometry totally in tune with the work. It must be remembered however that this formula is due less to his own preference (which was for no frame at all) and more to the prevailing fashion for white in interior decoration during the twenties and thirties. The Surrealists, who were fond of playing visual puns in their

Laetitia Yhap is a painter who often frames her own work in found materials, a tradition that has attracted many artists. The Guitarist (above) is framed in rope and sections sawn from a curved drawer.

paintings, also found room for such fun in their approach to framing, frequently deliberately confusing its role, inviting it to be both frame in the conventional sense, and a part of the narrative of the painting.

From a practical and technical perspective, two great developments in picture framing in the 20th century have had a stylistic impact as well as being technical advances. The first is the development of the aluminum or metal frames that were originally known as Kulicke frames (after their American inventor Kulicke), and the second is the use of plexiglass, not only as an alternative to glass but as a framing material in itself. Both materials were developed and became immensely popular in the 1960s and 1970s and endowed works (particularly the bold bright screen prints of the time) with a very satisfying cool crispness entirely in keeping with the contemporary fashion trends and designs. Metal frames were made and used in different colors, while plexiglass continues be used to great effect, particularly in making box frames.

Some artists will always continue to have some say in the presentation of their works, and some will no doubt continue to construct their work as an integral part of their frame, thus thwarting all attempts to wrest them apart, while

others will be content to let their works speak for themselves with no frames at all. Picasso drawings have been framed to great effect in simple silver frames as well as in ornate black-and-gilded 18th-century Spanish frames, both of which he would probably have approved of. The English artist John Bratby actually had a label printed with instructions proscribing the use of any frame that might encroach on any part of the painted surface of the work. He recommended the use of minimal battens fixed to the outer edges of the canvas. In the event, however, many of his paintings have ended up in elaborate gilded frames in keeping not with his wishes but with their presumed worth to their owner!

Symmetrical and oddly shaped canvases are another feature of the 20th century, and they too tend to invite minimal framing, partly because by their very nature they commandeer the space around them in a proprietorial way, throwing off the need to be framed.

Robert Delaunay is just one of the many 20th-century artists who picked up on Seurat's example and continued their paintings deliberately onto the picture frame, as here on the frame of Window Picture *(left).*

Four classic 20th-century formats (below) complement the primary colors and stark design of these abstract works: simple white battens, a white box frame, a molded clear plastic showcase for the assemblage and no frame at all for the circular work.

Charleston farmhouse in Sussex was the center of the Bloomsbury Group's decorative work (left), where they lived out their idea of an aesthetic encompassing the whole living space.

The Gluck frame (below) was designed and patented in 1932 by the artist Gluck. It represented a serious attempt to integrate paintings into the overall design of a modern interior.

THE ART
OF FRAMING

IN A WORLD WHERE ALMOST EVERYTHING
WE BUY IS MACHINE-MADE AND MASS-
PRODUCED, THERE ARE FEW AREAS OF
LIFE WHICH AFFORD US THE PLEASURE
OF COMMISSIONING SOMETHING MADE
BY HAND. THIS LUXURY IS STILL AVAILABLE
IN CHOOSING A FRAME FOR A PICTURE.

A strong image needs to be matched by a mat and a frame of equivalent strength. In contrast to oil paintings and other original works of art, decorative prints may be framed with room colors and furniture in mind.

At a good picture framer, you will have a wide choice of shape and finish of frame and color and texture of mat to select from, and it is your decisions which will determine the final result. Although machinery is of course used in producing frames, much of the process is still done by hand, so there is discretion for you and the framer to incorporate variations and details by choice. Arriving at the correct result takes time, patience, and careful thought, but the end product, a made-to-order picture frame, will be unique and should afford you pleasure for many years to come.

It follows that you should give some thought to what you wish to achieve before you visit the framer. The first principle is that it is almost always right to choose a frame that brings out the best in the picture rather than merely suiting a particular decorative scheme. A work of art framed to go with a specific color or pattern alone can look spectacularly ill-suited when, sooner or later, you find you are hanging it in a different context. It is also worth considering your own response to the painting. So for example a picture bought for its dramatic impact will dictate a frame that emphasizes this aspect and draws attention to the painting; a picture which is intrinsically contemplative and restful will require a frame that is low key, almost reticent.

Where pictures from an earlier period are concerned, thought must also be given to the possibility of finding a frame which is an original or reproduction frame of that period, or which, though modern in origin, makes reference to the earlier style. A little bit of research can be very profitable, and for this the History section in the first section of this book will give valuable help.

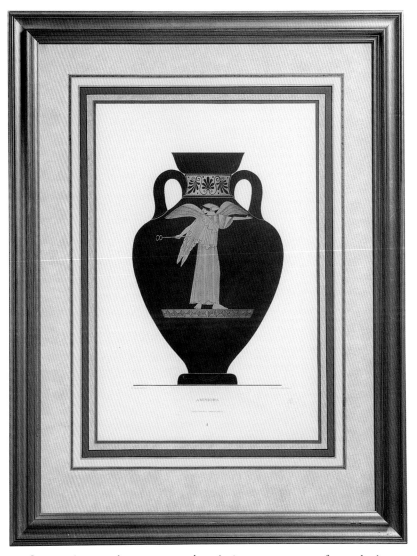

Some pictures however are by their very nature, framed almost entirely for decorative purposes; in this case the mat and frame can be planned together so the framing ensemble becomes a part of the furnishings as a whole. A scheme like this is best achieved by working with fabric swatches and color samples so the framer can aim at the closest possible matches. Some projects will require forethought: if you are proposing to hang a series of prints in a particularly restricted space, this will dictate the proportions of the mat and frame you choose.

OIL PAINTINGS, TEMPERA, AND ACRYLICS

In essence all painting involves the use of pigment combined with a binder such as linseed oil or water. In medieval times the normal binder was egg, and the resulting paint was known as egg tempera or just tempera. Though effectively superseded by the use of oil paint, tempera continues to be used intermittantly. For framing purposes tempera paintings are treated in the same way as oils, with one important technical proviso. Tempera needs at least a year to harden to the point where the surface will cease to be damaged by physical contact or dust. In this period the painting must be protected by glass or clear plastic, which must not come into contact with the paint surface. This can be done by placing a spacer or fillet between the glass and the work.

From its development in Flanders in the early 15th century, the use of oil paint spread gradually to Italy and the rest of Europe. Initially it was used in conjunction with tempera, but its versatile nature, combined with the development of linen canvas, meant that the use of oil paint on its own was widespread by the mid-16th century. However, oil paint is now rivaled in popularity by acrylic, a pigment bound in a synthetic resin. This was developed initially in Mexico in the 1930s by painters such as Diego Rivera (1886–1957), who sought a medium that would be more durable in paintings exposed to strong heat and light.

Oil paintings and acrylics can be executed on a variety of supports; wood; canvas, a generic term covering any fabric stretched over a wooden frame—the stretcher—but usually linen or cotton; paper or cardboard; and metal, usually copper. In the course of deciding on the frame, it is worth checking the support. Wood panels are susceptible to cracking or bowing, especially when the picture has been kept in a dry, centrally heated environment, and further damage should be avoided by "cradling" the board by gluing battens of wood to the back. This a job for a restorer and it is wise to find one, or choose a reputable framer who is known to provide restoring services.

Works on canvas are liable to become brittle, and as a result the paint starts to fissure, then crack and eventually detach. Dry atmospheric conditions contribute to this, but it occurs inevitably with time. Particularly severe problems occur when a painting has become damp, because of flooding or storage in a damp environment; cracking then frequently occurs as it dries out. The solution is to reline the canvas by bonding it to a new canvas, a task that should only be undertaken by a professional reliner. The process of bonding the new canvas is effected in such a way that the paint surface re-adheres to the original canvas.

Unless you are framing a newly painted work, this is also the time to consider whether your painting needs cleaning or any restoration. Once again, this is a job for a professional; amateur attempts at cleaning can easily cause serious damage to the painting, in particular by removing the colored glazes which can form such an important part of many older works. If the painting is very dirty, it is usually wiser to have it cleaned first and then to choose the frame; the change in the look of the painting after cleaning can on occasion be dramatic, with hitherto unsuspected details and highlights emerging, and this can influence you to choose a different, perhaps lighter, frame.

The two illustrations of the same painting show the dramatic difference effected by sensitive cleaning and restoration. Encrusted dirt and discolored varnish have been removed and the damaged areas restored. After varnishing, the painting is given more impact with a more generous frame.

The painting before restoration, sadly neglected, with color and detail lost and the canvas torn. Relining onto a new canvas is needed before cleaning of the paint surface can begin.

THE PROFILE
OF THE FRAME

Oil paintings are almost always close framed, with no mat between the painting itself and the frame. This means that the choice of frame is absolutely crucial, and the profile of the frame is as important a consideration as the finish. The close proximity of the frame to the painting means that the wrong shape or an inappropriate structural detail can easily distract the viewer's eye.

In the simplest terms, there are three basic frame formats. The most usual is that which leads into the picture, whether directly by means of a sloping bevel, or gradually by a curve inward, known as a spoon or hollow frame. The second general category includes those frames which extend on a level plane out from the painting. Included here is the shallower design of plate frame in which the outer rim is not noticeably higher than the inner rim. Then there are frames which fall away from the picture, either steeply or in a curve which may be concave (a reverse hollow) or convex (known as bolection). Within these types there are numerous variations.

There are no absolute rules about which type of profile is going to be most appropriate for a particular painting, but there are some general guidelines which can be helpful. Landscape paintings where the perspective is important generally benefit from frames that lead into the painting, as do portraits where there are background details such as a room interior or a view out of a window. In contrast, works in which there is no perspective element can work well with a reverse profile; this is often very successful with flower paintings, still lifes, and portrait heads. Flat-effect frames are often suitable for modern works; their simplicity and lack of reference to historical styles often recommend them to the artists and to those who favor a clear uncluttered effect.

An important additional element in the profile of the frame is the slip. This is an inner frame or flat section, usually smaller than the main frame, which produces a visual break between the frame and the painting. Slips can be in gold or silver, or may be painted or covered in linen, canvas, velvet, or other fabrics. Most frequently used to introduce a lighter or plainer element next to the painting, especially where the main frame is in a dark finish, slips can also serve to introduce a color that refers to an element in the painting which needs to be emphasized. A slip can also perform a structural function; a bevel slip within a reverse profile frame may be necessary to introduce some element of perspective.

Another factor to consider is whether the overall look of the frame is to be angular, hard-edge, or severe or, on the other hand, rounded and therefore softer in its overall effect. A formal portrait may well be best served by a frame with an angular, slightly architectural molding, where an informal looser painting with fluid lines in the composition will sit better in a frame with a more rounded profile.

Just as important as the finish on a frame is the profile—the shape of the molding in cross section.

The ends of each of the moldings in this selection of frames have been cut square to indicate the difference in profile. The ribbed gold frame is a classic hollow; resting on it is a reverse hollow, with a bolection molding to its right. Above these are two moldings designed to achieve a more or less flat effect so that the frame extends out on a level plane with the surface of the painting.

GOLD FRAMES

Overwhelmingly, gold has always been and still remains the favored frame finish for paintings, especially those in the western tradition. Its warmth and mellowness in close conjunction with the painting is its main advantage. It also catches and reflects light onto the work. There are relatively few paintings in which the colors and tonal values utterly reject gold as a complement; in a sense, as an "abstract" color it provides a neutral demarcation between the colors of the painting and the space outside the frame.

The "gold" on frames takes a number of different forms and it is worth getting to know the distinctions, as the look of the various types of gold finish varies enormously. At the cheaper end of the scale, you will encounter a wide array of mass-produced frames on which the finish is applied with gold paint or a metallic film made from alloys with no gold content. The techniques for producing these finishes have become very sophisticated, and the results are often very satisfactory, far removed from the bright and obviously

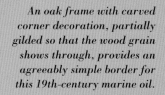

An oak frame with carved corner decoration, partially gilded so that the wood grain shows through, provides an agreeably simple border for this 19th-century marine oil.

metallic frames that at one time were all that was available. The quality of the alloy leaf has been progressively improved to the point where factory-made moldings with a finish known as copperleaf are almost indistinguishable from real gold leaf; they can provide a convincing substitute at considerably lower cost. The surface of these frames needs a seal or varnish to retard tarnishing, so the frames are often more resilient than real gold leaf; the drawback is that in the long run some tarnishing usually does occur, resulting in a dull, lifeless appearance. It is, however, a reliable guide to assess how closely the frame section resembles real gold leaf; the nearer the resemblance, the more likely it is the frame will continue to look good over a period of time.

For paintings of value, the alternative is a hand-finished gold-leaf frame. In the section on gilding on pages 140–43,

The deep colors of this modern painting (above) are balanced by the frame—gold leaf on a red bole base. The lines of brighter gold appear where the sheets of gold leaf overlap so that none of the bole shows through. This banding is characteristic of true gold-leaf gilding.

The inner frame on this tempera of the Palazzo Dario, Venice (right), is set into a flat panel; both are gessoed and toned white. The outer frame, in a manufactured gold molding, is constructed so that glass can be used—essential while the tempera hardens.

you can see how labor intensive, time consuming, and skilled this process is. Naturally, the resulting cost is much higher than that of factory-made frames, but there are profound advantages. The look of real gold leaf is in the end the most luxurious effect you can achieve, both because of the quality of the gold itself and because the process of preparation produces a much softer effect on the frame.

If you have a painting from the 19th century or before, you should also consider the option of framing it in period. When you have access to an antique frame dealer or a framer who can source period frames for you, it is worth trying to match your painting with an appropriate old frame fitting in period and character. (*The History of Framing* chapter will give you a good guide as to what to look for.) Auction houses now hold sales devoted entirely to antique frames, and this is another avenue to pursue. Your search will take time and patience, however; heavily decorated frames with complex molding along each length cannot easily be cut to fit your painting, so you will be looking for something of the correct size as well as style. Frames with continuous regular decoration or with molding at the corners only can be cut to

The formality of this frame (left), with its strongly geometric crossband decoration and squared corner detail with floral motifs, forms a counterpoint to the fluid subject matter of the painting. The finish, in bronze powder on a red bole base, is quiet and subdued. A canvas slip forms a neutral bridge between the image and the frame.

The light clear tones of this painting of kohl-rabi can sustain the bright effect of the oil-gilt frame, though the linen-covered slip affords an essential moderating element.

size and the joints masked by a frame restorer, or if the difference in size is small, the insertion of a slip can solve the problem. Of course, antique frames are expensive, and at times you could find yourself having to pay as much again for the frame as the painting is worth, but the consolation is that such frames are likely to hold or increase their value.

If you cannot source an old frame, consider the possibility of a reproduction. This is a perfectly respectable option, since copies of earlier styles have always been made, particularly in the case of 18th-century French patterns. Handmade reproductions are produced by specialist framers, and in some circumstances, for example where your painting is of non-standard dimensions, this will be your best route to a period-style frame. Mass-produced reproductions are also made, generally in standard sizes. These are usually much less expensive, but they are seldom finished with water-laid gold leaf—the surface is normally oil gilt or powder gilt. They do not have the luxurious feel of real gold, but carefully toned they can look very satisfactory.

Gold frames work well in combination with color, and sometimes the style of a particular painting will be better suited if the solidity of the gold is tempered by colored elements. On simple moldings it may be that a clearly defined area is colored; thus the concave section of a spoon or hollow frame or the convex part of a bolection molding is often colored, with only the inner and outer portions of the frame gilded. On a frame with plaster decoration on the other hand, the raised parts of the decoration might be gilded and the background rendered in color. This is a particularly appropriate choice for 20th-century work. An interesting variant can be employed where a simple effect is sought by edging a painting with a narrow gilt or color beading, placing it against a painted or gessoed panel, and then enclosing the panel itself in a larger gilt frame.

An all-silver finish would have been too heavy on this painting with a 1920s flavor, so a light wash of complementary color has been dragged onto the engraved center panel to highlight the pattern.

Although originally devised for works on paper, metal frames can also suit modern oils. This silver aluminum frame with a flat or brushed finish supplies a neat minimal edge to the painting.

ALUMINUM AND SILVER FRAMES

For certain paintings a silver frame can prove to be the most appropriate, sometimes the only, solution. This is very occasionally the case with earlier paintings, but by and large it is only an option to be considered when a 20th-century work is concerned. The look of a silver frame is cool, often severe, but there are certain colors to which this effect is well suited—these include pure pinks, grays, and blues and minty greens. Abstract works will often demand silver frames. It is best to keep an open mind and assess what suits the painting, rather than rejecting silver out of hand in anticipation of problems when you come to hang it.

Silver finishes vary enormously. In ready-made frames, the look can be bright and clear cut, which is often suitable for modern work, or toned with gray or sepia to produce a more mellow effect. Hand-finished silver frames are produced in the same way as gold-leaf frames. The bole can be red, which tempers the coldness of the final effect, or blue, gray, or black. The leaf can be real silver, though this does produce a metallic look, or white gold which is an alloy of silver and gold, which creates a gentler result. At the other extreme, there are the possibilities offered by modern aluminum frames. These frames come with profiles which permit them to be fitted on canvases, a useful way to solve the problem of paintings which require an absolutely minimal hard-edge framing treatment. Of course, aluminum frames themselves also come in metallic finishes other than silver, for example gold and bronze, and also in colors.

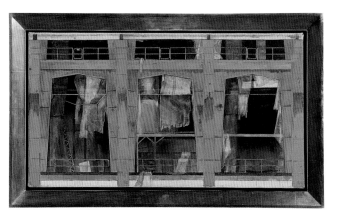

Silver frames particularly suit paintings with clear fresh colors such as vivid blues and greens, and can also tone down hot colors. Here a simple bevel-shaped frame finished in silver leaf serves to offset the warm orange hues in the painting.

The diffuse effect of this delicate mother and child study was created by fusing colored glass powder onto steel. It is admirably served by the softly contoured silver-leaf frame.

The dark background in this painting of flowers virtually dictates a black frame. Black has the added advantage of making the colors more vibrant. The decorative details in the frame allude nicely to its 16th-century Dutch and Flemish ancestors.

PAINTED FRAMES

For modern oils and acrylics, a painted frame with little or no gold detail will often be the ideal solution, either to achieve maximum simplicity with a very pale finish or to make a statement with a particularly vivid color. More complex effects can be achieved by employing the paint finishes familiar to us from the world of interior decoration (see pages 132–39 in *The Craft of Framing*). But it is as well to be cautious with these more dramatic effects. On the right painting, especially on works of a bolder or more decorative nature, a strong paint finish can be perfect; inappropriately used, such frames can draw too much attention to themselves and fight the subject matter of the painting.

A dark frame may be necessary where the painting itself is executed in dark tones, since a light frame might appear to jump out at the viewer or simply overemphasize the somber nature of the painting. A dark frame, ideally combined with a gold- or light-toned slip, will help to bring out and flatter the painting. Alternatively, a monochrome solid color may on occasion be exactly what is needed and it has the virtue of being relatively simple to achieve. But it is not the only way to produce a dark frame. A useful approach is to try a black frame with an undercoat of a different color which is "pulled through" the top coat slightly to give more interest to the finish. Blues and greens are possible but often the most successful base colours are red-brown or ocher.

Paint effects are used in a subtle, carefully considered way on this small oil of a village in southern France (left). The frame, two broad flat moldings, stepped with a gilded sight-edge, is finished in blue-gray broken with a spattering of buff brown.

A successful combination of gold with black. Although an all-gold frame could have worked, the black central band serves to sharpen the structure of the painting.

This Australian Aboriginal painting (below) needs no frills. A simple float frame with a narrow coloured border is the ideal solution.

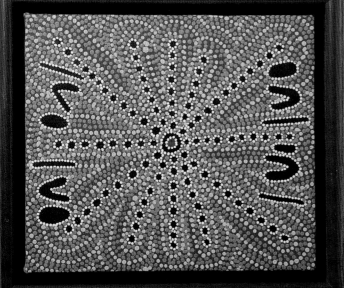

A sensitive approach is needed when using broad areas of color for framing. The dominant hues in this small head and shoulders portrait, deep magenta and black, have been carefully avoided in favor of a subsidiary color, somewhere between blue and green.

NATURAL
WOOD FRAMES

Recent years have seen a return to popularity of frames in plain unstained natural woods. Lightly sealed or polished, they are an excellent solution for framing modern work. Oak and ash are easily available, but it is also possible to obtain moldings in sycamore, beech, and poplar—all of these possess elegant appeal once the grain has been brought out by a varnish or wax finish. In flat or only slightly curved profiles, these woods make excellent frames for abstract work, either close framed directly onto the canvas or in the form of float or box frames. Where available, ramin, with its absence of grain, provides an even simpler, more clean-cut finish. Oak and ash work well in larger frames with more elaborate profiles, while a different look is obtained with pine, since the knots produce a rougher, rustic effect, useful for paintings which are more primitive in style.

Another way to use natural woods is to pickle them or wash them lightly with transparent color. Pickling, which has been in use as a finish for centuries, is now produced either by applying pickling wax, which gives a soft sheen, or by brushing on a light coat of diluted white paint. Sanded down when dry, it gives a softer effect than the wax. In either form this finish is suitable for a wide range of modern paintings, but especially those in which quieter pastel tones are the most predominant. Color washes, particularly in pale gray-blues and greens, are useful if you wish to highlight a specific tonal element in the painting. Whether white or colored, however, the point of these finishes is to show the grain of the wood through the paint, with the rougher areas of grain catching and retaining more tint than the smooth.

Pickled and pale finishes on polished wood can also be combined advantageously with other types of molding, such as wood painted in darker solid colors or stained, for example by inserting a pale color-washed or pickled slip between the frame and the painting.

The pale bleached tones of this landscape of Greece, executed in thinned oil paint, are balanced by a frame in pickled oak with an inner slip frame painted in a neutral watery green.

For this painting the artist, Laetitia Yhap, has used strips of wood from a boat as the border, making a maritime link between the subject of the picture and the frame.

This broad frame (near right) with a flat center panel is in plain, unstained oak, finished with a clear wax polish to a warm yellow-brown glow. Next to it (far right) is a thin, simply rounded molding in cherry, less commonly used for frames than other wood. It has a natural warm reddish color.

Pickled oak (right), produced by lightly washing or waxing the wood, is suitable for modern works. Pine molding (below) is valued for its rustic appeal, produced by the characteristic knots. Ash (below right) is similar to oak in color, but with a cleaner-looking, simpler grain.

Sporting and equestrian subjects were traditionally framed in walnut veneer frames with some gold detailing. The figured grain of the veneer and its rich color provide an excellent border, as in this copy of an early 19th-century painting of a foxhound.

VENEERED AND DARK WOOD FRAMES

There is a wide range of subjects and of hanging situations for which dark wood frames, with their effect of gravity and masculinity, are a natural choice. In subject matter, marine paintings and equestrian and sporting subjects come to mind, as do portraits, especially those in which the sitter has been portrayed in a formal manner. From the perspective of interior design, dark frames hang well in juxtaposition with traditional dark wood furniture and in more formal rooms, such as libraries or studies.

Oak, ash, pine, and so on can all be stained to darker colors of brown, and of course, traditionally this was how they were normally finished, especially in the case of oak. Some woods, such as mahogany, come naturally in a dark color and only need slight toning with tinted beeswax to bring them up to a good finish. The finaished effect is always handsome and sober, in contrast to the mellow effect of an all-gilt frame. If the look is too somber however, it can also be tempered by including a touch of gold in the form of a slip—a useful device.

An altogether richer feel can be achieved with veneered moldings. In England and North America there has been a tradition since the 18th century for using maple veneers, especially for framing sporting subjects. Maple veneer, when new, can have an unpleasing orange-brown appearance, but this mellows and darkens with time. The figuring in the grain of the veneer at times has small circular patterns within it, producing the attractive and desirable effect known as bird's-eye maple.

For marine and equestrian subjects, walnut veneer is particularly suitable, either over the whole area of the frame or in conjunction with gold; this can be at the sight edge alone or on both the inside and outside edges of the frame, with the veneer forming a central panel. Burl walnut veneer (formed from sections taken from the base of the tree) has a closer, more convoluted figure in the grain, creating a busier but more luxurious effect. By contrast, rosewood veneer, which has a darker purplish color, has a closer, more or less uniform grain; rarer than other types of veneer, it is traditionally used for miniatures and other small-scale paintings, applied to shallow beveled moldings.

Mahogany comes naturally in a dark color; here it has been enriched with tinted beeswax polish to complete the effect. A narrow gold slip has been used as a visual break since the background to the sitter is also in somber tones.

This amusing primitive painting of a pig has been complemented by a roughly carved rustic wood frame, stained to a dark finish.

An early 19th-century engraving of Paris is transformed by careful conservation work. The acid discoloration has been removed, revealing the subtle colors and wealth of topographical detail. The gold frame and washline mat in the French style complete the transformation.

VUE DU QUAI St BERNARD.

VUE DU QUAI St BERNARD.

WORKS ON PAPER

If your watercolor, print, or drawing is dirty or damaged, you should have any restoration work carried out before you decide on the frame. It can be worth seeking out a paper conservator or a framer who offers conservation services as a part of their business. Discoloration of the paper, staining, foxing, and "burn marks" resulting from the pine backing boards frequently used on old picture frames, can all be dealt with by a trained conservator. Often the paper is glued to a board and must be carefully removed before it is washed to get rid of the acid discoloration. Attempting these processes yourself is ill-advised; they demand considerable expertise.

Framing works on paper requires an approach which differs in a number of ways from that required for oil paintings. Works on paper are more fragile than paintings on canvas or panel and so they must be protected by glazing. In most cases, however, the glass should not come into contact with the surface of the artwork, and this brings in the second element to consider, the need for a window mat. Mats create the necessary gap between the glass and the artwork, performing a practical as well as an aesthetic function. Poor quality framing materials can damage the artwork, so you need to give thought to the conservation requirements.

For most purposes ordinary 1/16-inch clear float framing glass is the appropriate glazing material, unless a very large picture is being framed. In that case, for the sake of safety, your framer will advise a thicker grade of glass, but this increases the weight of the picture and may well dictate a heavier frame; the alternative in this event is perspex or plexiglass, clear plastic sheeting which is considerably lighter and is virtually unbreakable. But there are disadvantages; the surface of plastic is easily scratched. It also produces static electricity, which rules it out for pastels and charcoals; even the journey from the framer to your home will detach an unsightly film of pigment.

Ordinary glass and plastic will not protect your artwork from the harmful effects of light, so if you have a work which may suffer from exposure to ultra-violet light (a particular problem with watercolors), you should consider conservation or museum-grade glass or plexiglass. Incorporated is a UV-reducing component or filter which gives greatly increased protection, without affecting the way you see the picture. Be wary of using nonreflective glass or plastic. To achieve their purpose, these products refract the passage of light so the quality which removes the reflections also obscures the picture. This effect operates only very slightly when the nonreflective glass is placed directly against the surface of the picture, so it is an acceptable option for posters and reproduction prints, but when there is a gap between the glass and the picture, the distortion increases.

If the picture is pressed up to the glass, a number of problems can occur. In particular, humidity changes in the atmosphere can cause moisture to become trapped inside the frame, and this will damage the pigment of the picture. If photographs are placed against the glass, heat even from sunlight can cause the two to bond together. The presence of a window mat curtails all these problems and gives scope for additional aesthetic contributions. If for some reason a mat is undesirable, the same practical result can be achieved by inserting a fillet under the rabbet of the frame.

It is vital however that if the artwork is to be kept in good condition, only mat board of conservation or museum quality be used. Historically, all mat board was made of untreated woodpulp, which contained acidic residues harmful to the paper on which the drawing or painting was executed. In time, these unwelcome chemicals cause serious staining and progressive deterioration of the structure of the paper. In extreme instances, the paper becomes so brittle that it eventually starts to disintegrate. Professional paper conservators can save works on paper from further deterioration, but the processes are painstaking and costly, and rarely result in a complete return to the work's original state. Acid-free board is now widely available. It is not necessarily much more expensive, and should always be insisted on for work of any merit.

During the 19th century a vogue arose for surrounding watercolors with gilded mats. This remains an option, particularly where the colors have retained their strength.

WATERCOLORS

Watercolors are paintings executed in pigment which is bound together in a water-soluble medium, usually gum arabic. More generally used for sketching or recording, whether as the preliminary sketch or as the outline over which the oil painting was then continued, watercolors began to be viewed as paintings in their own right from the early 18th century on, although experiments in water-based media had been pursued by Albrecht Durer and other German painters from the early 16th century. Initially they were painted in the monochrome grays and sepias used for sketches, but by the mid-18th century watercolorists were employing a full range of colors.

The distinguishing feature of this medium as opposed to oils or acrylics is its transparency. The painter uses the paper to create effects of light and achieves differences of tone by adding more or less water to the paint. Watercolor can however be rendered opaque by the addition of white pigment, and in this form it is known as gouache or bodycolor; in contrast to the British School of artists, this was the favored way of using water-based paints in France, Italy, and elsewhere in Europe.

In its pure form, watercolor is a delicate medium, and the frame and mat should respect this. The simplest solution is to use a mat in a pale tone and a gently shaped frame finished in gold, perhaps with shot-edge decoration. This is always a good choice for framing traditional watercolors , especially with the mat left plain or given a single line of watercolor around the opening, or perhaps a light application of gold color to the beveled edge. Cream or off-white are usually appropriate but pale grays, gray blues, gray greens, buff, and sand colors can also work well; a mat much stronger in color is almost always a mistake with traditional watercolors.

A traditional solution for a delicate watercolor portrait from the mid-19th century. The rounded corners and shot-edge decoration of the frame, which is French from the same period, provide a gentle border, completed by the lightly washed mat with its gilded bevel. Miniature portraits, sympathetic in style to the main picture, are attached to the fabric hanging strap—a very pleasing group.

An alternative simple treatment is to use a double, or stepped, mat. For this, two mats are placed one over the other with ¼ to ½ inch of the inner mat showing. Normally the inner mat is in the same or a slightly lighter color, which helps create a greater impression of perspective. This is also a useful device where the paper of the watercolor is darker or has deepened with time; in this case the outer mat itself should also be slightly darker in order to balance the tone of the paper color.

Early watercolorists adopted the practice of surrounding their work with a band of color on the paper itself, usually in sepia or another subdued tint, to define the boundary of the painting. Out of this grew the formula of decorating the mat with a line and watercolor wash border, known as a washline mat. The possible variants of this form of mat decoration in color, tone, and format are endless. A wash border with a stronger colored line on each side is perhaps the simplest arrangement, but more lines may be added, of varying colour, strength and thickness. An additional element can be introduced in the form of a strip of gilded paper on the inner edge of the wash. Another subtle touch is to run a slightly lighter wash of color over the whole area of the mat board beyond the washline.

The washlines are applied by the framer, by hand, once the mat is cut, so there is enormous flexibility in what can be achieved. But it is as well to observe certain guidelines. In

The classic English treatment for a watercolor landscape (above right) is a generous mat decorated with a full line and wash border and a gold watercolor frame, here with shot-edge detailing.

This strong still life by Geraldine Girvan, with its bold use of color, needs an equally positive approach in the framing. Close-framing in a brightly gilded frame, with a narrow gessoed slip, gives vibrancy to the painting.

A double or stepped mat will often be the answer where a simpler effect is sought. Combining a middle-tone outer mat with a narrow inner mat in a lighter color leads the eye into the picture. The frame continues the simple theme with its painted finish in blue-gray dragged over an umber base.

particular the size, strength, and complexity of the washline should always be appropriate to the watercolor itself and should never overwhelm it. If the first thing you notice is the washline decoration, then the balance is wrong. It is also advisable to choose a color for the wash border which is not a dominant color in the painting. So, with a landscape where greens and blues predominate, choose a subsidiary color, say sand or buff, for the watercolor wash and allude to the dominant colors in the lines that surround it.

There is no reason why you should not extend the mat decoration to the device of the double mat. In this case the two mats are cut in such a way as to leave ¾ to 1 inch of the inner mat showing and this is then decorated either with a gold paper band or with a narrow washline. With this treatment the outer mat can afford to be in a stronger color altogether, as it is safely distanced from the painting by the lighter inner mat.

Whatever mat decision you arrive at the choice of the frame is also vital. With traditional watercolors, gold is almost always the classic solution. Paintings from the 18th

The frame on this abstract painting (below) illustrates how silver can provide an obvious and elegant solution for a modern work in which blues predominate.

A modern gouache framed by the artist (above). The exciting colors of the painting are enhanced by the bright white mat which is bordered by a rough wooden frame. The lengths of molding are joined with overlap corners rather than miters.

or 19th centuries usually look best in an old frame or a good reproduction and, failing either, a modern gold-leaf frame. Works from the early and mid-20th century can also be well suited by pale wood frames, natural polished oak or ash, and frames with a pickled finish. But the black and dark stained wood frames in fashion in the first twenty years of the 20th century in many countries now appear unduly gloomy.

Modern works can permit a much more adventurous approach. Silver can be suitable to complement paintings where cool colors predominate, or to tone down bright pinks. Painted frames can also be especially effective, either with a paint finish throughout or combined with gold or silver. The frame profile is not so important as with oils, unless you are close framing, in which case the same general rules apply. But the tonal relationship is still important. Bright gold or silver may work on a strong painting, but choose something more reticent for a delicate work.

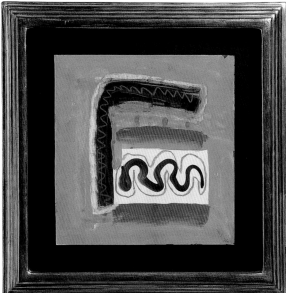

A combination of a chunky bright gold leaf ridged frame and a jet-black cardboard mat serve to give this gouache and mixed-media work maximum impact.

The contrasting effects of four different mat solutions on a modern watercolor of a gondola in Venice, starting with the classic washline mat (above left). The effect is traditional and gentle.

A reduced washline border will often prove more in tune with modern work, serving to break up the plainness of a pale mat with just the minimum of decoration (above right).

With watercolors, as with all works on paper, you must consider the proportions of the mat. As a general guide, a picture up to 6 by 8 inches needs a mat of about 2½ inches; up to 16 by 20 inches about 3 inches; up to 24 by 32 inches about 3½ inches, and above that 4½ to 5 inches or more. But whatever size of mat you have, the bottom edge should always be slightly greater than the other sides, or in any event than the top edge. This is necessary to counteract an optical illusion which makes the top edge appear heavier. With a horizontal painting the bottom edge should be only slightly greater; thus 3½ inches on a 3-inch mat. With a vertical painting, rather more at the bottom, say 4 inches, may be appropriate. It only becomes unnecessary to observe this rule if for some reason (for example, if the space where you intend hanging the picture is limited) you choose a mat of 2 inches or less.

In a few cases a mat may not be the appropriate route. This might be for practical reasons. For example, if the watercolor is very large, a substantial frame of 2¾ inches or more without a mat, but with a slip or fillet to provide the necessary airgap, can be a sensible choice. In this instance, adding on a mat of the right proportions could well increase the glass size and weight to such an extent as to create a serious problem when you come to hang the picture. There

can also be aesthetic reasons for having a frame only—close-framing as it is known. Small-scale watercolors or gouache which are very intense in color may well be set off better by a generous size frame and no mat.

A particular framing dilemma can sometimes arise with 19th-century watercolors, usually in the case of those works that were originally executed in strong colors. In the middle of that century, a vogue arose for surrounding watercolors with gold mounts, often in real gold leaf, perhaps to give them more importance and status when they were hung together with oil paintings. However, if the watercolor has faded over time, the mat, if still bright, may now look overwhelming against the paler colors of the painting. Conversely, if the gold on the mat was of poorer quality and has become tarnished, it will now look drab. The natural reaction is to substitute something lighter, a washline mat perhaps, and this is usually quite appropriate. But beware—if your 19th-century watercolor is valuable and it still has its original gold-leaf border in good condition, the original mat and frame may together constitute a good part of the value of the complete artwork. Even if you change them now, it may still be worth keeping the original frame and mat and storing them so that they can be reunited with the painting later if necessary.

Darker colored mounts intensify the colors in the painting (above left). To heighten this effect, the opening of the mat has also been brought in slightly and a red chosen to emphasize the warmer tones of the work.

An alternative use of the double mat (above right) reverses the usual formula. Instead of leading in from mid-tone to light, a much darker color is used for the under mat, creating the effect of an inner frame. The strong narrow line of blue draws attention to the linear elements of the painting.

Using the mat with the sparer wash border, a silver and blue frame has been selected to work in with the predominant blues, greens, and grays of the watercolor.

PASTEL PAINTINGS

Pastels are sticks of color composed of powdered pigment held together by gum. First devised in northern Italy at the end of the 16th century, they achieved their most widespread popularity in the 18th century, particularly in France where they were commonly used for portraiture. Once applied, the color does not change, so the overall effect can be judged immediately. Pastel rests on the surface of the paper and can be easily dislodged or smudged. Fixative can be applied to prevent this from happening, but it has a dulling effect and is best avoided except as a light film; some artists however follow the practice of fixing the pastel painting when it is almost complete and then adding highlights on top.

If you have commissioned a pastel, say a portrait, or have bought one unframed, it is vital to get it framed as soon as possible, before any damage can occur. A generous gap between the painting and the glass is always advisable and this can be achieved by using a thick grade of mat board, a double mat, or by increasing the distance under the glass (the airgap) by inserting a fillet in the rabbet of the frame. As with watercolors the mat may be decorated with a washline border or painted overall in watercolor with just a

narrow border left light at the inner edge. An alternate approach is to use a double mat. The special papers made for pastel painting are often Canson or Ingres papers in gray or buff colors and they have a slightly textured surface. If the artist has covered the paper closely, with pastel the normal process applies of choosing a mat by reference to the colors of the painting. But if areas of the tinted paper show, the picture can be made to look somber with a light mat, even though the colors of the pastel may themselves be fresh and bright. In this situation a darker mat on its own would look heavy so the solution is to use a double mat with a light inner board and a middle-tone or darker outer board balancing the paper color.

The intensity and brilliance of pastels can sometimes make them suitable for close framing. Ideally, you should choose a frame which is substantial to make up for the fact that there is no mat. A gold, silver, or painted slip under the

The strong white areas in this pastel suggest the use of an off-white mat alleviated by a washline border. Instead of gold, a painted gray frame has been chosen to work in with the colors in the work.

The intense color of this painting (above) virtually demands a dark mat. A rich red brown is lifted by a light inner edge with just a simple decorative band of antiqued gilded papers.

glass provides the necessary airgap or you can have a dark fillet inserted under the rabbet; the latter option can be particularly useful when the pastel is unfixed since it permits any fragments of pigment which do detach to fall onto the fillet at the bottom and rest there without disfiguring the look of the frame.

It is worth mentioning small oils on paper and oil pastels since they present similar practical and aesthetic problems as those of pastels. Like traditional pastels, oil pastels come in stick form but are bound in oil and come in stronger vivid colors, producing an effect nearer to that of oils on paper. Because paper does not provide the firm support of canvas or board, it is normal to put oils on paper under glass and in any event glazing serves to enhance the look of the picture, often lending it a jewellike air. As with pastels, it is best to provide a generous airgap with a thicker grade mat, a double mat, a slip, or a fillet. If you choose a mat it is worth opting for a middle-tone or dark color. With a thick mat the pale area showing on the deeply cut bevel gives an accent of light at the edge of the picture; with a double mat the inner mat in a light color performs the same function. But another solution, particularly appropriate to oils, is to have a narrow gold or silver slip between the mat and the painting itself.

Close framing works well for oil pastels. A somewhat larger frame will be needed, as if one were dealing with an oil. Here a gold outer frame with an inner frame colored in gray dragged over red is employed to complement the colors of the still life. A narrow gold slip has been inserted to keep the glass off the surface of the pastel.

Dark mats should be used with caution with drawings but here a matching rust red Japanese paper has been employed to good effect to work with this sanguine study after Fragonard.

At the opposite extreme, this shows the same drawing with a plain cream mat, inscribed with the artist's name and date, and an unaffected polished oak frame; this style is well suited to a collector.

Jean Honoré Fragonard
1732 – 1806

DRAWINGS

Here the drawing is given an historical treatment with a typical French washed mat in blue with sepia line and gold decoration (above). The antique Louis XVI baguette frame with carved moldings has a watergilt finish.

If the drawing is to hang with a collection of varied works, including watercolors, a conventional washline treatment is perfectly acceptable (above right). The decoration has been kept delicate, however, and a frame chosen in a simple polished wood with marquetry inlay.

Many contemporary drawings and the overwhelming majority of drawings from earlier periods are preparatory in nature, representing a stage, sometimes one of many, in the artist's completion of a painting. As such, their spontaneity should be treated carefully, and it is a safe rule to avoid very elaborate, over-decorative mats and frames. This is not to say certain solutions, such as colored mats, should be discounted, but that a careful sense of balance should be employed so as not to overwhelm the subject matter.

In fact, colored mats were traditionally used for drawings and it was normal, particularly in France from the end of the 17th century onward, to mount drawings within a blue wash border with some gold and ink line decoration. This complemented the sepia or sanguine coloring of such drawings particularly well, but it is also a very rewarding treatment for pencil drawings from the present day. At the other extreme, drawings are always well served by a simple mat in cream or off-white, depending on the paper color, and it is this solution that is often preferred by serious collectors. The use of plain mats can serve to unify a collection of drawings varying in style, medium, and subject-matter. A mat with a decorative border such as a washline can be appropriate, especially if the drawing is to hang next to

watercolors or other works of art in a different medium, but care should be taken to make sure the wash border is delicate and does not introduce a distraction. A particular effect of colored mats should be noted; darker colors emphasize the linear element in a drawing, while mid-colors draw the eye more to the tonal aspects. As always, the primary rule applies, namely that a frame which seizes the attention of the viewer before the work of art it encompasses has failed to perform its true function.

Similar considerations apply in arriving at the choice of frame. Historically, the frames used for drawings were narrower and less decorated than those employed for oil paintings. Although still elaborate to modern eyes, such frames were considered simpler at the time, particularly in juxtaposition to the ornate furniture and decoration against which they were hung. In France, the baguette frames used for drawings throughout the 18th century provided an elegant and restrained style of frame, especially suitable for conte and chalk. In choosing a modern frame, elegance and restraint remain as the ideal guidelines. Uncomplicated gilt, veneer with a discreet amount of decoration, perhaps in the form of marquetry inlay, or plain waxed oak or ash, provide the best frames to complement drawings.

This pen and ink drawing on fine transparent handmade paper defied conventional framing attempts. The solution was to set it against a pale board and frame it close in an elegant copper-leaf molding.

A brooding industrial landscape executed in compressed charcoal (below) needs no more than a generous pale mat and a flat frame stained to a deep charcoal gray.

CHARCOALS AND PEN AND INK DRAWINGS

Darker and heavier than pencil drawings, charcoals need different, rather more positive treatment. The delicacy required for pencil sketches or finished pencil works can simply look too weak against the strong black lines and shading in a charcoal drawing. The same is often true of pen and ink drawings, where the line is firmer and sharper.

The aim as always is to balance the strength of the drawing with the weight of the frame ensemble. This can be achieved by putting on a middle or dark-tone mat combined with a simple frame; in this case the mat provides most of the weight to create a balance. Or use a larger, perhaps more elaborate, frame with a pale mat with wide borders; this is often successful where the charcoal is dramatic in its effect. Alternatively the impact of a charcoal can be enhanced by an altogether different approach: setting the charcoal back within a dark deeper frame with little or no mat. Setting the charcoal back from the glass has a practical advantage in that charcoals which come into contact with the glass at any point can leave a deposit on the inside surface. If not recessed in a box frame, they should at the very least be put behind a double mat, or a mat with a thick bevel. This ensures a safer gap between the surface of the drawing and the glass.

Pen and ink drawings, although usually lighter in weight than charcoals, still require more in the mat or frame to balance the strong line and tone of the ink. Black frames and pale mats are often the first solution to test, but as with charcoals, consider middle-tone or dark mats and more substantial frames than would be used for pencil works.

A Venetian red inner mat under the main mat in silvery gray provides a subtle accent of color on a charcoal nude in a black frame with embossed decoration.

More elaborate solutions sometimes pay off, as with this reproduction copy of a charcoal by Georges Seurat. The 19th-century style swept frame enhances the intimacy of the drawing, which is bordered with a pale green French washed mat.

The ink in this 19th-century French cartoon has faded over time, so a quiet lightly washed mat has been used with an inner ivory mat to lead the eye in. But to avoid too bland an effect, the frame has been finished in color— dark ox-blood red and gold.

A "macaroni" was a dandy in 18th-century Britain. Frankly, this gentleman (below) does not need much elaboration, so a mahogany veneered frame and a blue-washed mat are ideal.

THE HOUNDSDITCH MACARONI

Cartoons by the English painter William Heath Robinson contain so much detail, and in this case strong color also (above), that the best option is a broad pale mat. The reeded gold frame provides a nice element of restrained decoration.

CARTOONS AND CARICATURES

After the delicate restraint of pencil drawings and the somber force of charcoals, a contrast occurs with the more lighthearted use of the medium. Cartoons, caricatures, and illustrative drawings permit on occasion a more imaginative and uninhibited approach to framing. From the riotous watercolors of Rowlandson to the sinister world of Charles Addams or the saucy and colorful seaside cartoons of Donald McGill, it is the unexpected elements of the genre that invite originality in framing. Of course the framing should not compete; as always the primary focus remains the artwork itself. But the challenge is to include something in the framing or mat which draws attention and excites interest. Boldness in the overall framing treatment usually pays off with all humorous art, attracting the viewer's attention to the picture. At its simplest, this can mean just placing a small cartoon in an oversize mat to make sure that it is not passed by. Or it can mean enlivening a black-and-white humorous drawing with a particularly vivid color line in the mat. Washlines can be punctuated by a space to display the humorous caption. Even the frame itself may be of a specially striking color to pick up an important element in a colored drawing or print.

Where there is a caption or joke, it is important that this be included in the framing. If the artist's original written words are still in good legible condition, they should, if at all possible, be displayed, possibly in a separate window. Otherwise the mat itself should be inscribed with a good printed or handwritten rendering of the caption.

This is a light-hearted caricature, and the framing is in the same vein. A vivid yellow mat distracts the viewer from the sorry state of the background paper, while an unusual eye-catching note is provided by the lined black and cream frame.

The cartoonist H. E. Bateman experimented with the idea of the strip cartoon in the early years of 20th century before it became the common device it is today. This mat has been cut with three openings to show the strip and the handwritten caption under the main drawing, but a wash border has been used to make the point that this is really a single work of art.

Sometimes a firm black frame provides the best border for a cartoon, as here where it serves to emphasize the design and colors of this modern work by Annie Tempest (below).

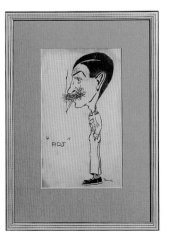

SPECIAL TREATMENTS

A category which will often benefit from a more adventurous framing approach is that of paintings which take their theme from the theater, ballet, and opera. The drama and color contained in many set and costume designs can be translated into the frame and mat and the paintings will often stand up to strong treatment. Mats covered in fabric, especially silk, are a good choice, and a strong vibrant color picking up an element in the design can prove highly successful. Some designs still carry swatches of the fabrics proposed for the costumes and these can provide an excellent starting point. But there are pitfalls here, particularly if there is a dominant color in the picture. This might be the color to pick up on, but if it forms a dense mass, such as the whole area of a dress, it can be oppressive to repeat it in the mat; better to seek out a subsidiary color.

Consider mats covered in handmade papers, such as Ingres or Fabriano papers, or the Japanese or Indian papers which provide a different choice of colors. Another approach to try is that of exotic multicolored wash borders. By this method it is possible to pick up on a number of different elements in the design. The choice of colors and the way in which the mat decoration is arranged will need careful thought, since the combined effect can easily become over-elaborate or confusing. On occasion, though, an outrageous effect may be exactly what you want; some of the primitive 19th-century theatrical prints of popular actors and singers can be ideal candidates for strong treatment.

Boldness and inventiveness can be carried through into the choice of frame—perhaps with a plaster moulded decoration or a color finish. Black in the frame is ideal if there are strong black or charcoal linear elements in the picture. Certainly if the mat is relatively plain you can opt for an elaborate frame; this will prove most successful with set designs in intense colors. It may even be a good idea to treat the work as an oil and close-frame it in an antique or reproduction frame.

Mats made from board washed in a strong color, richly decorated with strips of specialist papers, or covered in fabrics such as silk (left), provide an excellent accompaniment to works of a more exotic nature.

Boldness and imagination combined to produce this highly original proscenium arch frame for a theatrical print (below). The finish mirrors the tones of the print, while the curtains wittily replace the conventional slip.

The aim with this set design has been to achieve an unashamedly decorative effect in the framing, from the gold-covered bevel, sponged and stippled border, and blue-washed board to the antique gold-leaf frame with leaf design plaster molding.

EARLY PRINTS

The term print nowadays covers two entirely separate fields, and it is vital to understand the difference before making an approach to framing. The original meaning of the term was confined to works produced in relatively small editions by the early printing processes such as wood-engraving, copper engraving, and etching, and variations of these methods such as mezzotint and aquatint. Larger print editions became possible with the development of lithography and steel engraving in the early 19th century. All these processes are still used by artists to make original prints, that is, prints that are produced by the artist alone or in collaboration with a print technician, in genuinely limited editions.

Nowadays, the term also covers the images which are mass produced, sometimes in thousands, by commercial printing processes. These "prints" possess little or no resale value so framing options can be considered with less concern for preserving their condition. With original prints the opposite is the case, especially true of old master prints and all the early prints dating from the mid-19th century or before. The value of these prints varies according to rarity and to condition. In particular where the paper is fully intact, it should not in any circumstances be cut or folded as this may drastically affect the value. Even if it has already been cut it should ideally still be framed without further trimming. On no account should any cut or fold be made

within the platemarks; this is the indented line around the image left by the impression made by the metal plate from which the original engraving or etching was made.

Old prints should ideally be mounted within an acid-free window mat, as for drawings or watercolors. If the paper borders around the images are large, this will necessitate a very wide mat. In this case serious collectors often favor a plain cream or white mat. But a pleasing alternative can be a double mat with a generous pale-toned inner mat decorated with lines or a line and wash, surrounded by an outer mat in a slightly darker color. With colored prints, washline borders are appropriate. A chalky blue and sepia decoration can also be a successful solution with monochrome prints that are themselves sepia in color.

If the print has already been trimmed, close framing is another option. Ironically, this was a favored way of treating prints in the past when considerations of value did not apply. When close framing, a wider frame is usually required than when framing with a mat. In the past, prints which were framed without window mats were simply sandwiched between the glass and backing board. With prints of value, especially rare handcolored works, it is advisable from a conservation viewpoint to make sure that a card fillet or spacer is placed between the glass and the print to distance it from the glass.

This engraving has been given prominence by being placed within a very broad double mat. The inner mat is bordered by roughly executed sepia lines to create the effect of an inner frame.

If you want to frame an old print in period, gold or black are not the only choices; this elegant polished wood frame with brass corner details (right) is in period style and can easily be imitated.

The black and gold Hogarth frame was widely used on prints in the 18th century. Derivations are easy to come by today. This variant in a pleasing oval shape (below) is from the 19th century.

The pale subtle coloring of this lithograph needs a gentle touch. The two fine gold frames with, between them, a bevel slip lined in cream silk, lead the eye in without creating a distraction.

Here the formula has been to keep to the cream and gray tones of the print with a deeply beveled ivory-colored mat, punctuated by a single pale gray line, and a frame in blue-gray with gold edging.

ARTISTS' PRINTS

With 19th- and 20th-century artists' prints much the same considerations apply as in the case of old master prints. In contrast to mass-produced decorative pieces these prints are hand produced in relatively small editions using the same techniques—woodcut, engraving, and etching—as the prints of the 16th to 18th centuries. They are original works of art produced with care and technical expertise by the artists themselves, and the ideal way to approach them is to treat them as though they were contemporary black-and-white drawings or watercolors.

Black-and-white prints with strong lines or dark shaded areas will be well suited by black or dark gray frames, and just as with charcoal drawings, it is worth looking at broader frames in wood stained gray to a deep charcoal finish. Prints where a fine and delicate line predominates will repay a gentler approach: fine gilt or silver or a light color. Mats can be in a medium color such as gray or gray-blue, although, as with all serious works on paper, cream or off-white should always be considered first. For large prints, where a wide paper border already provides a clear border to the image, a very satisfactory solution is to lay the print against a card so that the deckled edge of the paper is shown. Then, as a border, use a box frame with a deep rabbet and a generous fillet of at least ⅜ inch between the glass and the mat board so that the print is recessed within the frame.

This strong black-and-white woodcut of a town in Bosnia (above) has the intensity of a charcoal drawing. A simple dark gray frame, lightly varnished, and a plain cream mat, prove the best solution.

The rich golds and inky blues of this color etching seemed to demand a slightly unusual frame, in the same coloring, set close on the print border with no intervening mat.

A light green and gold sponge painted finish, avoiding anything overly decorative, provides a feel of restrained luxury in the frame on this lithograph of a nude figure (above).

The disparate architectural details in this print (above) are brought together by a strong black frame.

ARCHITECTURAL PRINTS AND MAPS

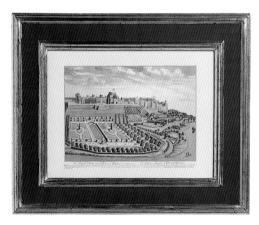

Verre eglomisé, glass painted on the reverse side in black, has traditionally been used for prints, and it is combined dramatically here (below) with a black frame with a gold sight edge.

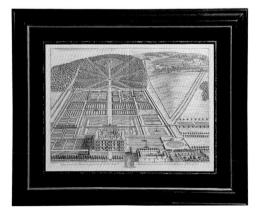

Architectural and topographical prints provide a perfect opportunity for you to be bold and experimental with mat colors and decoration and with the proportions and finish of the frame. The larger prints especially have the potential to play a dramatic role in any decorative scheme, and the framing needs to be considered with this in mind. Their effect is usually to create an air of formality and grandeur, so be prepared to opt for mat board which is rich in color and frames which are impressive.

Dark-colored mats are particularly appropriate both with black-and-white and with colored prints. Bottle green, burgundy red, Prussian blue, even black can be tried; it is not unusual either for relatively bright colors to succeed, especially with monochrome prints. Color can be provided by ordinary mat board and there is a vast range to choose from, but you can also look beyond the commercial brands of board. Specialist papers with more exciting textures can be laid onto plain mat board and wrapped around the bevel;

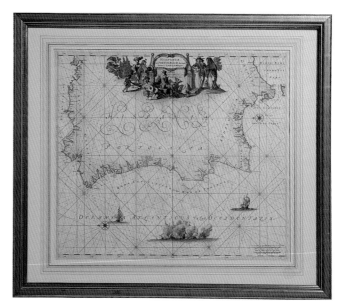

oriental papers, particularly handmade Japanese papers, are a good case in point, offering a variety in hues which are altogether different from North American and European products. An interesting avenue is to use fabrics such as silk or linen. Once again, there are types of manufactured boards with fabric already laid on, but a good picture framer should also be able to glue down a material of your choice on the mat board. The only drawback is that decoration cannot easily be applied to fabric mats, though this can be overcome by using the device of a double mat. Probably most luxurious is to wash over the entire board in watercolor or gouache, either in a single color with some gold decoration near the sight edge for example, or with a wash border in one color, surrounded by a complementary color extending over the rest of the board.

For the frame, the first possibility is of course gold. If you already have an old gilt frame in good condition it should be retained; replacing the faded or stained old mat with something fresh and more interesting will frequently bring the old frame back into its own. But new, generously proportioned frames in an antiqued gold finish or in gold leaf work well in conjunction with colored mats.

Often a good choice will be a black frame, especially with black-and-white architectural prints. All-black frames however may be too somber. Black frames combined with gold or black finishes which have other color elements, a warm undercoat or a tinted finish, usually have more life and interest to them. Other paint finishes may be appropriate. Dark green or red frames can look dramatic, although it might be better to exercise restraint in the choice of mat; a

Two maps with contrasting treatments: the delicate coloring of the map of Spain (above right) is matched by the washline mat and a quiet copper-leaf frame. Dark green, frequently used for the coloring in maps, is also very suitable for the mat; the subdued gold frame accords with the buff tones in this map of Portugal (right).

Close framing in gold frames with a central section in deep blue makes a decorative statement on these two colored prints (left).

middle-color mat with a washline might suffice here. The imitation finishes such as marbling or fakewood are also worth considering.

Smaller architectural and topographical prints will benefit from similar treatment, though scaled down. An alternative, often used with prints of architectural details, is to combine two or more prints in one frame, with the mat cut with two or more windows and maybe an outer mat to unify the ensemble. If you have a set of small-scale prints this solution may allow you to achieve a more interesting hanging arrangement than with numerous individually framed pieces.

Colored topographical prints—landscapes and town views—have more in common visually with watercolors and a similar approach is called for in the framing. Perhaps not as dramatic as black-and-white architectural subjects, these prints will usually benefit from the more restrained washlines and gold-leaf or wooden frames that would suit watercolors of the same subject.

Maps do not usually have the same bold compositional force as architectural prints, so slightly different criteria apply. Dark mats are an appropriate choice as are washline and other decorative treatments. Many old maps do however possess a color border as part of the print, and in this case it can be a mistake to repeat this feature in a washline, especially if the existing border is strongly colored. For the frame, the range of choice is similar, although as a general rule the proportions will need to be smaller than in the case of architectural subjects.

Achieving a stunning effect with the combination of image and frame is a priority with decorative prints, as here with this bold red, black, and gold frame on a rich oriental-style interior.

In the past carved "rope" decoration was often incorporated into frames for marine subjects, and this tradition has been revisited here for a print of boats and sea monsters. The rope detailing is picked out in gold, balancing the strip around the sight edge.

This frame takes its cue from the blue detailing in the image, but uses the decorative feature of the bamboo effect in the inner section to give added interest.

DECORATIVE PRINTS

Apart from architectural and topographical subjects, there is a vast variety of decorative prints available, with subjects ranging from flowers, seashells, fish, and animals to costume prints and fashion plates, from food prints to hot air balloons, ships, and cars. In addition there are all the 19th-century prints of classical subjects and of genre scenes such as "Street Cries," that show street sellers hawking their wares. Old bookplates are another rich source of highly decorative images, especially illustrations from classic children's books.

Originally produced as engravings, these prints were mass produced from the middle of the 19th century on, thanks to the discovery of the lithography which meant much longer print runs could be made. Their modern equivalents are almost always printed by photographic methods, which allow for virtually unlimited quantities to be produced. Decorative prints are now one of the most popular choices for framed images. For anyone starting out, they are the most accessible form of artwork available —at the bottom end of the price range, they are far less expensive than any original painting might be. And for the specialist collector, there is also a fine choice of 19th-century original aquatints and engravings. Catering to this increasing demand, many framing galleries now deal purely in decorative prints.

Crackle finish is a very useful device for decorative frames, used here with panels in blue which give a nice impression of movement.

When displaying sets of prints, it is sometimes better to rein in the decorative impulse, especially if the pictures are to hang in a block. Here an off-white gessoed mat affords a gentle lead-in from the subdued gold leaf and hand-painted frames. Fleurs-de-lis are used as corner motifs—highly appropriate for botanical prints.

As the name implies, the prints can be treated primarily as an aid to decoration, so the colors of the room in which they are to hang are as much a guide to the choice of print as the colors in the print themselves. (Sets of prints are a favorite formula with interior decorators for this very reason.) The subject matter can also be a factor; decorative prints can be themed to suit a particular location, so that botanical prints are chosen to hang in a conservatory, for example, and a collection of food pictures in a kitchen. Personal hobbies and enthusiasms can be reflected: pages taken from old illustrated catalogs showing collections of sport equipment or fashion plates are very popular.

The options for framing these prints are as diverse as the subject matter. They can of course be treated in a similar manner to watercolors, but this is an area where you can usually afford to throw off restraints and be adventurous. In particular, colorful and extravagant mat decorations come into their own. When choosing the mat and frame, fabric swatches and color samples are helpful, though it can be a mistake to try to match colors exactly; a more interesting approach is to find a color in the print which can be tied to a secondary color in your decorative scheme by means of the mat or washline.

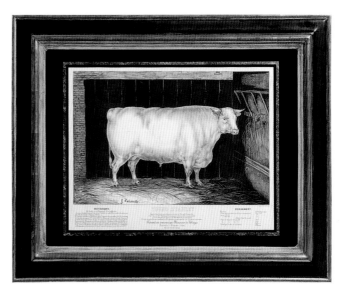

These 19th-century French lithographs have the traditional border known as verre eglomisé. Gilt strips are applied on the reverse side of the glass, which is then painted black. The ensemble is completed by the gold-leaf frames with black painted centers. The history and descriptions of the cows are included with the images for added interest.

In addition to using colored mat boards and applying straightforward washline borders, you could treat the mat more unconventionally with paint techniques such as stippling, sponging, or stenciling. In place of the central area of color in a washline border, strips of marbled or other strongly patterned papers are very effective, and the same papers can also be used to cover the inner board in a double mat. (Numerous suggestions for decorative mats can be found on pages 128–29 of *The Craft of Framing*.)

One device which has a long history with prints, from the early 18th century, is black and gold glass, otherwise known as *verre eglomisé.* This is glass painted on the reverse side in black, which replaces the need for a mat. Often the glass includes gold decoration either in the form of a band of gold near the inside edge or sometimes as painted motifs. The technique, carried out by hand, can also show a caption or title below the print.

There is also scope for interesting effects in the frame. Veneered wood frames, in particular maple and walnut, provide a fruitful area to try in conjunction with decorative prints, as do marquetry frames with their patterned inlays. Painted frames can prove particularly apposite, whether finished in simple color washes or in a more elaborate fashion. This is an area in which added decorative details such as roundels at the corners of the frames and patterned slips often provide an interesting finishing touch. On occasion the frame may also be designed or decorated to include allusions to

This provides a fine example of an antique decorative frame. It is in carved wood with exaggerated center and corner decoration, regarded during the early 19th century, when this aquatint was produced, as being very suitable for sporting subjects. The broad gilded slip takes the place of a mat.

This delightful tortoise is so perfectly served by the tortoiseshell-effect frame that there is really no need for anything extra. Genuine tortoiseshell was originally used as a veneer, but paint effects mimicking the look soon took over and have been widely used for a long time.

This is another example of a wood frame of a type used from the 18th century on for racing and sporting subjects. The veneer most commonly used was maple, as in this case, and the usual frame shape was either the bevel profile shown here or a gently sloped reverse frame.

The handcarved frames on these two botanical prints from the 1750s (above) have incised floral motifs at the corners and are gilded over a red clay base. This finish is distressed and varnished for a lustrous effect.

This frame has refrained from being as overloaded as the traveling musician in the print, but has borrowed the warm brown-red coloring for its center panel. The gold stenciled flourishes in the corners allude nicely to the extravagant details in the print itself.

the subject matter of the print. Thus, for example, bamboo effects for oriental subjects, "rope" beading for marine prints, incised fishscale patterns for fish, and of course a tortoiseshell paint effect for turtles and tortoises. This is an area where imagination and inventiveness pay off. In contrast to the principles which apply to framing paintings, drawings, and so on, the aim here is to combine the image and frame in one package so that they produce an effect which is unusual and above all eye-catching.

Sometimes a particular print or the place where it is destined to hang may demand a frame with a more specialized, individual finish. Primitive paintings, whether genuine or faux naïve, often respond well to specially finished frames. Achieving effects of this nature successfully is not an easy thing to do. A good sense of design and a sure hand is required, and you will need to find a framer who is effectively something of an artist as well. If you have a particular motif in mind, say from an old pattern or ornament book, this can be taken as a guide, but remember that the best results will not be obtained from slavishly copying an example; you will need to trust to the framer's skills and judgment.

One of the simplest ways of applying the decoration is by the use of stenciling and this of course ensures a more predictable result. Stenciling has a long tradition, especially in early American framemaking, and is very suitable for primitive paintings. Stenciled designs can be applied as a continuous band along each length of the frame, or be used simply to decorate the corners and perhaps the center of each side. It is more of a challenge to create successful freestyle designs; this is where artistic skills are essential, and a rather more subtle approach. Thus freestyle decoration is often best applied not on the surface of the frame, as is usually the case with stenciling, but in an intermediate layer of the finish, with one or two washes of color or tinted varnish over the decoration to seal it.

Where colorful and highly decorated frames are chosen it will often be better to dispense with a mat. Mass-produced modern prints do not need to be distanced from the glass and close framing will achieve more visual impact.

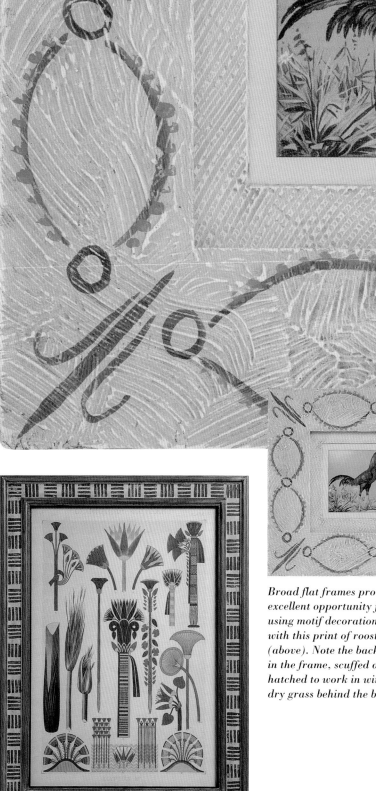

The colors and the patterns in this frame refer to the subject matter of the print without copying any one detail too slavishly.

Broad flat frames provide an excellent opportunity for using motif decoration, as with this print of roosters (above). Note the background in the frame, scuffed and hatched to work in with the dry grass behind the birds.

The broad ivory-colored scored wood frame strikes a sympathetic note on this classic French film poster from the 1930s. Dispensing with a mat and placing the gold-edged frame close up against the image gives it maximum impact.

POSTERS AND GRAPHIC IMAGES

Posters, characterized essentially by the juxtaposition of an image with some lettering conveying a message, form a specific grouping within the general category of prints. The combination of lettering and, very often, a strong visual image calls for a different approach. Usually, simplicity is the best guide. This way the poster stands alone and the frame merely performs a practical function.

The most basic method is to block mount. The poster is glued down to a board of the same dimensions, about ¾ inch thick, and is sealed with a protective coating, the edges of the board being painted black or another suitable dark color. This method is very effective in presenting the poster without any distracting additional element. Also, it does not involve glass so it may be a suitable choice in certain situations, such as a child's bedroom. Once it is glued down, however, the poster cannot be removed without damaging it,

The clear-cut design and coloring of this café poster from the early 20th century is well suited by the no-nonsense lacquered frame in a matching orange red.

Narrow frames in simple profiles are usually the first options to be looked at when tackling posters and modern prints. Colored lacquer finishes, plain silver or gold, wood or aluminum: the result is a spare, minimal effect ideally suited to the graphic quality of most posters and modern prints.

so block mounting should never be attempted with anything that is rare or potentially valuable. Almost as simple is the clip frame, a device whereby the poster is secured between glass and a backboard. Clip frames are easily available in kit form and can be assembled at home.

Aluminum frames are especially suitable for posters. The crisp shapes and metallic finishes of these frames work well with the combination of image and graphics. There is the added advantage that the strong systems that hold the frames together allow you to place a large-scale poster in a frame which presents a very narrow profile to the viewer. Aluminum frames also come finished in black and numerous other colors so the options now extend beyond silver and brass, originally the only colors available. Some brands incorporate a fillet to separate the artwork from the glass, useful for framing older valuable, and often delicate, posters. Modern prints, often executed in strong lively colors, respond well to a similar style of frame.

Wood frames with a color finish, whether in matte paint or high-gloss lacquer, offer a further option, as do plain polished woods. Almost always, the best shapes to go for are the simplest, either flat or slightly rounded. Moldings with more complex profiles tend to look inappropriate or even pretentious, except in those rare instances where the subject matter demands an elaborate response from the frame.

This modern screen-print with its strongly graphic repeat images is ideally served by a wide plain white mat and an aluminum molding. The scale of the image makes it appropriate to use a slightly wider molding than is usual; this one is 1¼ inches wide.

A calculated risk was taken with these two companion collages by the same artist, (left and far right on facing page). Frames identical in shape were chosen, but with differing finishes. This one, with its painted patched effect, is warmer to tone in with the red and sand colors of this piece.

COLLAGE AND MIXED MEDIA

Many contemporary artists work in more than one medium, combining watercolor, gouache, and acrylic with charcoal and pastel, and using collage and assemblage. The resultant works do not always fit into easily definable categories for the purpose of framing, and boldness and an open mind are both needed to achieve the best result.

In making the aesthetic decisions, the first priority is to pay heed to the overall look of the piece rather than to consider whether it is executed predominantly in any one medium. So, on the one hand, a work which is based on watercolor but with additional elements in, say, oil or oil pastel may well be strong enough to merit surrounding with

The strong shapes and uncompromising colors of this wine-inspired design asked for a frame treatment that was equally forceful; flat black lacquer with a vivid red inner frame coupled with the double mat in red and white provided the answer.

a substantial frame as if it were an oil on paper. By contrast, thinly painted oils with light pencil and charcoal elements can benefit from being treated in the same way as works on paper with a mat and a delicate frame.

Collages and assemblages will often need to be put into box frames or mounted with double or triple mats to make sure that the parts of the work which stand out from the surface of the paper or canvas do not come into contact with the glass. On a practical note, it is worth remembering that glazing is almost always essential to protect these works, both from casual damage which can easily detach collaged pieces and from long-term atmospheric pollution. The latter is a particularly important point since conservation and repair work on collages and mixed media pieces frequently pose considerable problems to the professional restorer.

A subtle collage comprising a selection of Spanish labels is best suited by a treatment that pays attention to its quiet coloring. The frame is painted in soft greens and the mat washed in yellow-buff watercolor.

This collage (above right) has very different colors from its companion (far left on facing page). The frame and mat seek to acknowledge and at the same time contain the predominance of acidic yellow and green.

ORIENTAL WORK

This broad description covers an enormous array of paintings and prints in various media and styles from a number of different cultures. The appropriate framing will be equally varied in nature and not necessarily all that different from the treatments suitable for work from the western tradition. Most of us will be familiar with the sight of a delicate but slightly faded Japanese print enclosed in a shabby narrow black frame. In the west, this was always the classic way of framing these delightful works. But if prints are to be hung individually a mat is helpful to lend them more importance; it also gives protection. A simple cream or off-white mat is usual so as not to interfere with the colors of the work; a more interesting variation is to have a mat covered in neutral

silk or Japanese paper, which comes in naturally produced colors more suited to the tones of the prints than those of commercial western mat boards. For the frame, branch out from plain black to simple dark polished woods such as cherry, or to lacquer finishes in dark reds, greens, or blues.

There are two categories of oriental work that present a framing challenge. The first is the scroll painting. An easy solution is to respect the natural format and hang them loose on the wall, but this is not always the answer, especially in cities where atmospheric pollution will pose a problem. Where the work is of little value, the scroll sticks can be removed and the painting framed in the normal way under glass. The alternative solution, essential where the scroll is of value, is to frame the entire piece in a display case.

At the opposite end of the scale come the small colored paintings on rice paper that were produced in China from the later 19th century on. Painted with western tastes in mind, they depict animals, birds, fishes, boats, and genre scenes. The paper on which the paintings were executed is particularly delicate so careful handling is essential to avoid damage. A pleasing variant to consider for both Chinese and Japanese works, and for Buddhist tankas perhaps, is a frame with rounded corners—in Japan, picture framers have traditionally made frames in this manner. A framemaker who can produce ovals should have the machinery and skills to achieve what you want. A different challenge is presented by works from the Indian subcontinent: that of strong color. Be prepared to consider similar colors for the mat to those found in the paintings themselves.

For these two paintings a framing formula has been chosen which places all the drama at the center by setting the works within a confined area of strong color surrounded by a quieter mat and frame.

Indian painting presents interesting and challenging color combinations which need to be reflected in the framing. This rajah is thrown into relief by the backing board and slip covered in a hot orange Japanese paper.

These three Japanese prints from the early 19th century combine to form one image, so it was essential to find a framing solution that mounts them neatly in three separate openings, but makes the point that they must be viewed as one piece. The cream silk-covered mat, combined with the broad dark blue lacquer and gold frame, arrive at the right result.

Two uses of lacquer for Chinese paintings: the landscape (far left) is framed in a Chinese red lacquer with inlaid marquetry detail. A traditional black lacquer with gold decoration has been used for the 19th-century watercolor on pith paper (left). The dark frame is alleviated by the use of the yellow mat.

These small paintings of birds of prey are rendered more jewellike by being set behind glass in a polished wood frame (right) and an ebonized frame (far right).

This black-and-white print (below) is very small in scale, so a disproportionately wide mat has been used to draw attention to it.

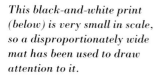

SMALL-SCALE PAINTINGS AND MINIATURES

The framing of small-scale paintings can pose a particular challenge. Although it is a general principle that the bigger the painting, the bigger the frame, the converse can apply with very small works. The rationale for this is that the frame is now called upon to give importance to the picture and draw the viewer's attention. This is especially important in the case of small paintings that are rich and intense in subject matter or coloring; a narrow frame in this case would almost certainly appear lightweight and stingy.

The generous proportions needed can be supplied by the frame itself, and you should not be apprehensive about using elaborately molded or complex frames if the work is strong enough to benefit from them. Alternatively, you can try an arrangement comprising a deep inward sloping slip, either painted or colored by an appropriately colored fabric such as silk or velvet, bordered by a narrow gold, silver, or dark wood polished frame.

An additional device with small paintings is to put them behind glass. In general, oil paintings are not glazed, since they are protected by a varnish which preserves them from atmospheric damage; also the reflections from the glass in close proximity to the varnished surface of the picture can

Making the most of a charming miniature of a lady in oriental-style costume (above). The oval painting is set behind glass within a completely flat rectangular frame gessoed and painted to mimic ivory veneer.

The combination of a very broad frame and an unusual painterly finish draws the eye to this modern portrait of a boy (left).

The principle that dark frames make dark paintings appear more alive was applied to this 17th-century miniature (right): the gold-leaf bevel is vital to reflect light into the portrait.

Light would have damaged these paintings (below) so a hinged frame was made. They can now be displayed on a table when desired and then stored away.

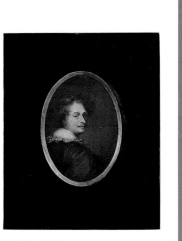

These two tiny paired paintings on ivory, of a Moghul emperor and empress (below), have been set together within a generous oval-cut mat covered in cream silk and then bordered in a simple frame painted an earthy red.

prove distracting. But small works can usually be hung in a position where reflections are not a problem and the glass has the effect of intensifying the impact of the painting. This is particularly successful where the combination of deep slip and narrow outer frame is used.

For circular or oval miniatures which are to be framed singly, the traditional treatment, or a modern variant of it, is often the most satisfying. This involves the use of a frame more or less flat in profile with perhaps a slightly shaped or detailed inner edge. An alternative is a "cuvette" frame with a flat outer edge that breaks to curve gradually into the painting. The finish of these frames can be gold, but most often in the past they were ebonized, sometimes with oak-leaf shaped hangers attached to the top, or they were veneered. The outside shape of the frame can be oval or round, following the line of the internal dimensions, or rectangular. Modern copies of these old styles are made, and they provide a good substitute, usually preferable to the bright mass-produced modern oval and circular frames. But it is also worth hunting for genuine old miniature frames, either via period frame dealers or by keeping your eyes peeled in antique and secondhand stores.

It is worth seeking out original frames for old family photographs. This 19th-century decorated frame with a gold oval spandrel (right), is typical of the sort of frame which was considered necessary to dignify the new art of photography.

The brass corners and decoration on this frame (far right), just as much as the portrait within it, denote its origin in India at the beginning of the 20th century. Its rustic and masculine style make it as suitable for its subject as the delicate design of the gold frame next to it is for a late Victorian lady.

PHOTOGRAPHS

In the early days of photography, elaborate framing was the norm, particularly for portraits, and examples may still be seen of decorated plaster-gilt frames with slips covered in dark velvet and lacy inner frames in bright gold leaf. The aim was both to emphasize the claims of the new art form to be considered as a serious alternative to painting and, in the case of portrait photography, to dignify the sitter. In addition to gold, dark polished woods such as oak and mahogany were used for landscapes, town views, and genre subjects as well as portraits. Where such frames survive, some cleaning and the application of good beeswax polish is often all that is needed to bring them back to life; 19th-century dark oak frames respond particularly well to this treatment and still provide an excellent surround for sepia-toned photographs.

If you do not have the original frame, then a modern equivalent in dark wood is probably the first choice. Modern gilt frames tend to look too bright in contrast to the faded tones of old sepia prints. The same is true of modern reproductions of 19th-century photographs. For the mat in either case, try pale colors such as deep cream, sand, or beige. If you do use a dark color such as bottle green, it is best to

Polished dark veneer frames often prove the most suitable choice for group portraits. The sepia tones of this charming photograph of brothers and sisters ranging in age and height are subtly matched by the sand- and sepia-colored double mat.

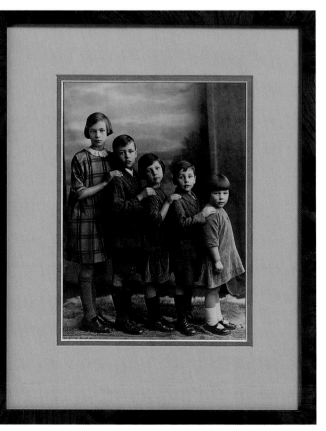

Oval frames work well
with head and shoulder
portraits. The antique gold
finish of this frame serves to
highlight the detailing of the
gold jewelry in this handcolored photograph.

A problem frequently
encountered is what to do
with large collections of old
family snapshots. Rather
than frame them individually
it can make far more sense
and prove more interesting to
group them together, as in
this multiple-window
treatment with a very
modern, clean feel.

Often the most suitable treatment for modern photographs is the simplest: a generous white or off-white mat, depending on the tone of the photographic paper, and a neat uncomplicated black or charcoal gray frame.

reduce the borders of the mat, as too much dark color around the photograph has a gloomy, deadening effect. Any mat decoration should be kept simple; on a light mat perhaps a solitary line of subdued color and on darker mats a single line of gold or a gold bevel.

Twentieth-century black-and-white photographs need careful and sensitive treatment. The classically used formula is a white or off-white mat of generous dimensions enclosed by a simple black frame. As a general guide, the tone of the mat should be no lighter than that of the photographic paper, for if the mat is brighter, the photograph can appear dingy. Where the photographic paper has discolored or faded, a gray mat may be appropriate, either light, medium or as dark as charcoal in tone; on occasion a black mat may even be the best choice. The other well-tried option for black-and-white photographs is an aluminum frame in silver, gray, or black. If a minimal clear-cut look is what you seek, metal framing is almost certainly the best way to achieve it. In particular, silver-finish aluminum looks good with either a pure white or a black mat. If silver looks right with the photograph, but you need a softer effect, consider wood with a silver or even silver-leaf finish.

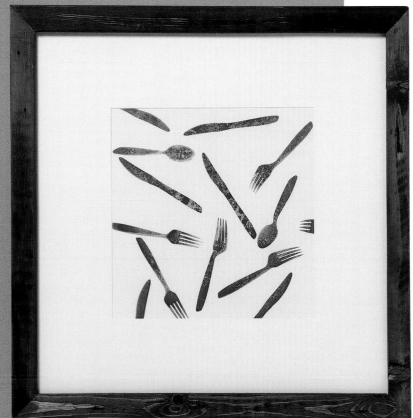

A rustic wooden molding has been used to good effect here on this unusual photographic still life study of flatware; an essential element again is the clear white mat.

Give thought to the option of grouping sets of photographs within the same frame. Here a look of absolute simplicity has been achieved with a bright white mat and the narrowest gauge of aluminum frame.

If the more usually accepted options do not seem to look right, return to the old formula of polished wood. Mahogany, rosewood, and other darkwoods, including figured veneers such as walnut and burl poplar, can prove surprisingly successful, provided you adhere to the same guidelines for the mat and choose white, gray, or black. Color photographs permit more latitude with the mat and frame. In addition to all the options for monochrome work, colored mounts can be a good choice. For the frame, simple gold can work well, as can colored frames, specially those with a lacquer finish. But one point to bear in mind is that photographs with a flat finish should not be put in a high- gloss frame; the effect will be to make the photo look dull.

Small photographs may need slightly different treatment. If you have a large number of snapshots on a particular theme, one possibility is to group them together within a large frame. Ideally, the photographs should be massed together in varied sizes so that none of the background board appears. If this is not possible, try to choose an appropriately colored board to show in the gaps between. Another route is to group two or more photographs in the same frame within a mat cut to provide a separate opening for each of them. This lends itself particularly well to groups of old family photographs. They do not all need to be the same size, but it is useful to have pairs of the same size so that an element of symmetry can be achieved.

For portrait photographs, an alternative is to put them in stand frames for display on tables or shelves. The classic display frames are either leather covered or silver, normally bought ready-made to fit standard photograph sizes. There is no reason why you should not commission a stand frame to be made in normal picture frame molding; a stand can be attached quite easily to the back of the frame. Polished veneered frames, including those with inlaid marquetry, can provide an attractive accompaniment, while a more inventive approach is to have a plain wood frame made, preferably with a flat profile, and to cover it with a fabric of your choice; velvet is very suitable, as are patterned fabrics with small-scale motifs.

The old formula of polished wood—oak, mahogany, or walnut, as here—still works well with modern photographs, especially with sepia work. Flat or shaped moldings are equally suitable, but gold details in the frame are best avoided.

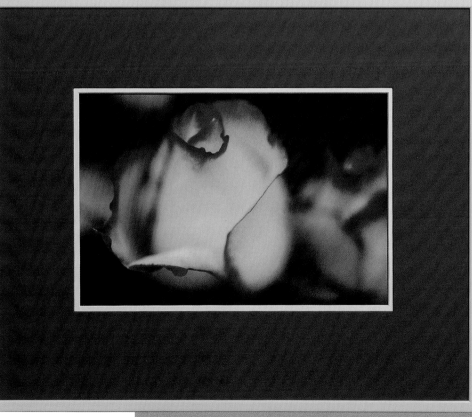

With color photographs it is worth trying strong colored mats. The colors of the rose make the red mat an obvious choice here but a pale inner mat has been inserted to provide a visual break.

OBJECTS AND EPHEMERA

Framing does not begin and end just with paintings. Beyond works of art in the conventional sense there are scores of other subjects for framing. Some of them were traditionally intended for hanging on the wall, needlework samplers for example, but there has been a growing trend in recent years to seek out more unusual subjects for display. Objects that were originally in everyday use, for example, given a creative framing treatment, can be turned into decorative pieces; a set of teaspoons with decorated handles or a favorite old pipe perhaps.

The first and principal category which comes to mind is that of fabric in all its forms. Needlework, embroideries, and tapestries have traditionally made excellent subjects for display, but there are many other samples of textiles that would be suitable for framing. Remnants from old materials used for curtains or chaircovers, for example, can make excellent framed images, especially fabrics with printed pictorial patterns such as *toile de Jouy*. Repeat images can be framed individually and hung as a block, or different sections of the fabric can be framed as one within different windows cut into a single mat.

Small sections of woven fabric taken from oriental rugs which have become too threadbare in places to be left safely on the floor are also prime candidates for hanging on the wall. An unusual method of treating pieces such as these is to frame them between two sheets of glass, rather than on a backing board, leaving a border of clear glass around the fabric. The background wall covering then effectively acts as a mat, so it is important that the rug sample matches the decor of your room. The glass must be anchored securely into the frame, of course, so you must choose a frame molding with a wide-enough rabbet for the hardware and sealing tape to be invisible when viewed from the front.

Even whole items of clothing can, with imagination, be transformed into impressive objects when they are presented within a frame—Chinese robes in rich reds and deep blues, embroidered vests and jackets, tribal garments and even designer dresses from this century. A plexiglass display case can be the best option for large items; the garment is secured to the back or suspended on a rod. Given a good hanging location, the result will be most impressive.

Another fruitful source of framing subjects is that of collections. Most of us make or inherit collections at some point in our lives. Stamps, cigarette cards, matchboxes, coins and medals, tiles, seals, butterflies, fishing flies, and so on all frame up well and have the added advantage of providing variety within picture-hanging schemes.

Variety can also be produced in another way. Many of the objects and ephemera discussed in this section lend themselves to framing in unusual shapes. The foremost example is that of fans. Traditionally these have always been presented in fan cases; recognizably fan-shaped box frames which are usually lined inside with silk in a color to complement the tones of the fan. But arrangements of objects—seals, for example—also look good in circle and oval frames, and all these odd-shaped frames prove very useful to add interest when it comes to picture-hanging.

Finally, a practical point. One of the principal reasons for framing, as we have seen, is to give better protection to fragile works of art. This consideration often applies even more strongly in the case of fabrics, objects, and ephemera. Many of these items deteriorate if left exposed to the atmosphere or stored haphazardly in drawers or boxes. Framing carefully and sensitively done can have the double advantage of allowing you to enjoy the pieces and of preserving them for the future.

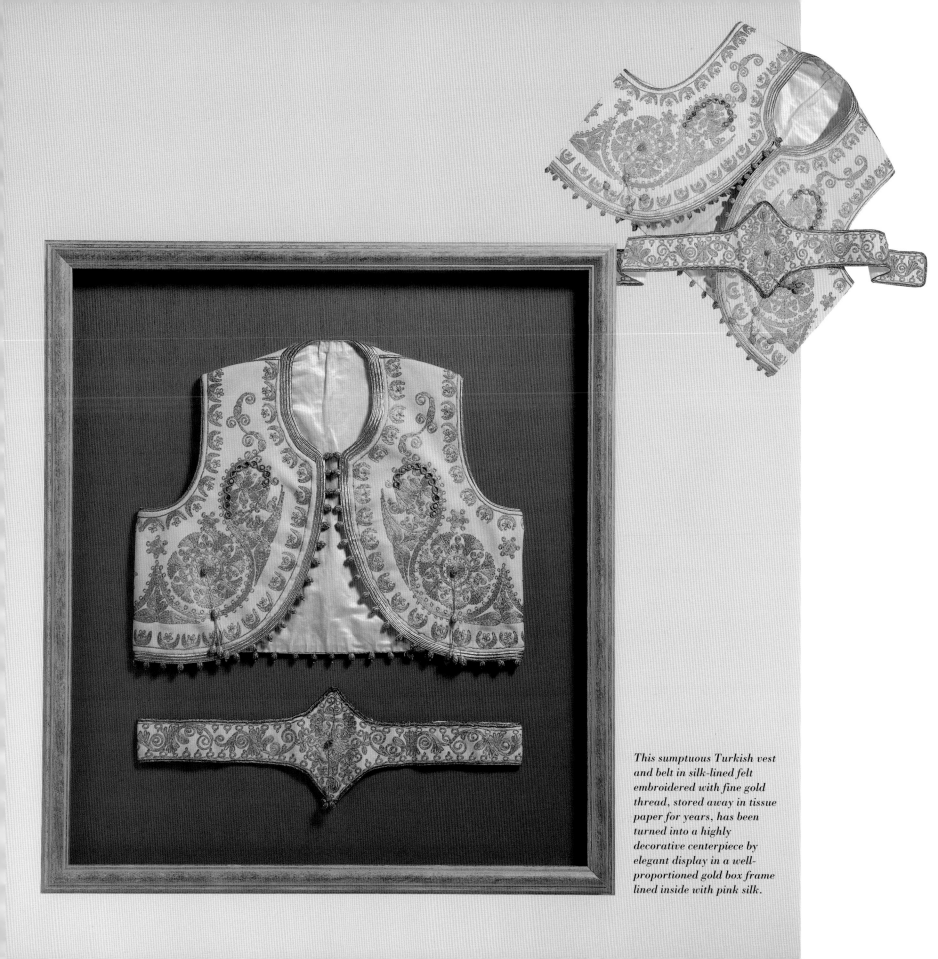

This sumptuous Turkish vest and belt in silk-lined felt embroidered with fine gold thread, stored away in tissue paper for years, has been turned into a highly decorative centerpiece by elegant display in a well-proportioned gold box frame lined inside with pink silk.

When framing fabric pieces it makes sense to use materials in sympathetic patterns to provide the backing or the covering for the mat. Under this delicate lace collar a deep blue background shows up the fine work, and a mat lined with pale blue ticking provides a decorative border. The fabric theme is continued into the frame with more fine blue ticking.

For this quilted sampler, a bright white mat has been selected to provide a stark counterpoint, and the decoration in the scheme has been relegated to the frame with its muted figuring and shell corner blocks.

FABRICS

The mounting and framing of fabrics is a rewarding area. But the choice of a framing scheme has to be thought about carefully and with imagination, so that the end result is both sympathetic to the particular fabric and decorative and eye-catching at the same time. For the framer the fabrics most usually encountered are various types of needlework, which their customers have created themselves or received from friends or relatives. Often these pieces arrive in a misshapen state and the first technical task is to stretch them over a firm backing so that they are presented as flat as possible in the frame. With a delicate work the best solution may be to sew it onto the backing or to use a thicker board and secure it with dressmaker's pins, but with more robust pieces, the edges of the fabric base can be glued onto the reverse side of the backing board. Traditionally the normal course then was to close frame it without a mat border, often in stained oak or in maple or rosewood veneer. The enormous variety of moldings if this sort now available allows a wide choice within this tradition, but it is also worth considering painted frames and gold or silver finishes.

To make more of the piece, however, you should consider a mat border. As a general rule, ordinary mat board on its own looks dull against fabric, and the best option is to select a sympathetic fabric, and cover the mat in it. This will be the normal course to follow when framing more exotic items. The more three-dimensional aspect of whole garments will dictate some form of box frame. A conventional frame with a fabric-covered slip or fillet inside, to raise the glass away from the garment, is one route to follow. The choice of the right fabric for the backing and the slip is of the utmost importance; framers cannot be expected to carry a selection to choose from, so it often makes sense to choose and buy this yourself if you want something unusual.

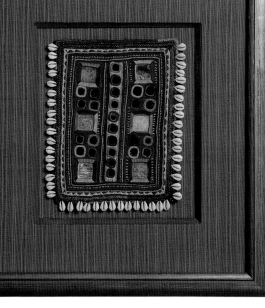

It is worth comparing the framing on this mirrored piece with the sampler (left). Here a much warmer, more enveloping scheme has been chosen. The piece itself does not stand out so clearly, but the overall ensemble is richer.

A model boat is presented in a wooden box roughly painted to resemble the insides of an old wooden vessel. It is surmounted by a frame made from flexible lead roof flashing, the dull metallic finish echoing the detailing on the model itself.

THREE-DIMENSIONAL OBJECTS

The framing of three-dimensional pieces, individually or, as is very often the case, in groups, leads us into a realm where an open-minded and innovative approach is a priority. Both in the construction of the frame itself and in its final appearance we are in effect moving beyond the world of the picture framemaker and into the spheres of the cabinet-maker and modelmaker.

Put simply, what is needed for most of these objects is a display box, and the challenge is to design a solution which develops out of this form of practical structure to produce an imaginative and decorative piece in its own right. In a sense, there are two different ways to tackle the problem. The first is to accept that a display box is exactly what the piece is and proceed on that basis. Coins are often treated in this manner; the simple wooden box in which they are presented aims to create a dignified, unfussy effect which carries reference to the sort of display cabinets one might see in an old-fashioned museum. Cases like these are often referred to as "shadow" boxes because the shadows thrown by the object define the three-dimensional relief and serve to further highlight the object itself.

The same sort of statement is made, but in an altogether different, more modern spirit, when objects are shown in a plastic display case. A five-sided plexiglass cover is fashioned from bent or joined pieces and it is mounted on a backing which can itself be made from clear plastic, for a completely transparent box, or from some sort of rigid board. The object is then secured in a suitable fashion to the back or to the top side of the cover, or simply placed on a support attached to the back. A good example of where this provides an excellent framing solution is in the presentation of puppets, with the string being taken up through discreet holes drilled in the top of the cover.

Collections of objects of varying sizes present a special challenge. The aim is to allow each piece to be displayed in its own right but for the frame to achieve a cohesive effect.

The inner frame, with neatly constructed compartments trimmed with brass dividers, isolates each item in an asymmetric pattern to engage the viewer's eye.

An original monochrome treatment for painted wooden eggs (above) marries them with fake fur. A stark frame and white mat concentrate the eye on the witty combination at the center.

The other route to framing solid objects is to treat the case much more as an extra-deep frame rather than as a plain box; this treatment allows for the introduction of all sorts of decorative elements into the border. These elements need not in themselves be complex. A model boat, for example, can be very attractively presented in a box surmounted by a frame in a simple molding finished with stains, distressed coloring, cracked varnish, and so on, lending a nautical effect. It is worth referring to the particular nature of the piece in this way by tying it in with the decorative details of the frame or using sympathetic materials. Another good example is where seashells are framed in wood which has a driftwood look. There is also the opportunity to try out more unusual materials that would not traditionally be used in framing, such as aluminum sheeting or lead roof flashing, or even something which injects a humorous note or a slightly kitsch element, such as fake fur.

The metal box frame in brushed aluminum matches perfectly this 1950s wind-up robot (above right).

The frame and arranged contents of this assemblage work, The Art Clock (right), were conceived as a single piece by the artist. The objects are unified by the aged wood of the frame.

Two contrasting, but both simple, shallow box frames containing ceramic works (right and far right). Here the pale tones of the flower have been carried through into the frame.

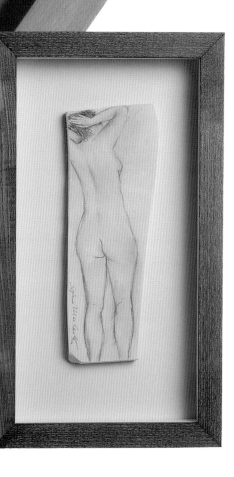

Here emphasis has been given to the line element of the delicate drawing on unfired clay by staining the frame to a smoky gray color.

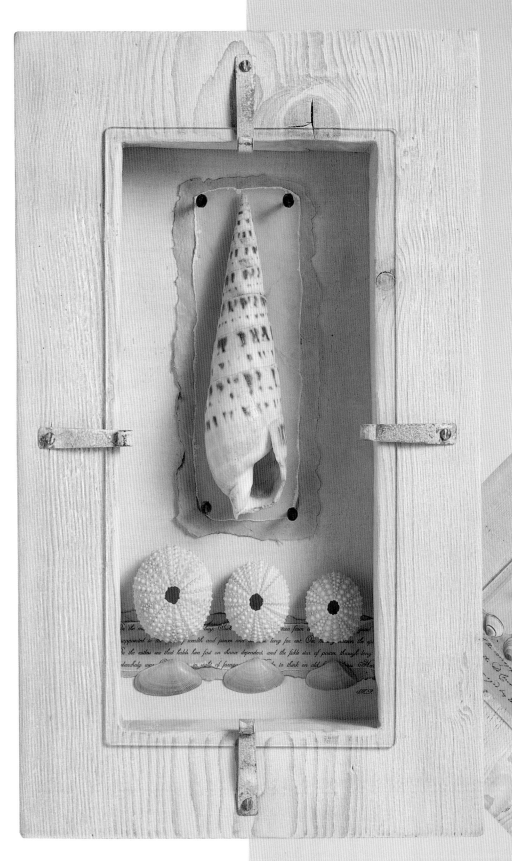

By using very pale bleached pine as the frame material on these shell boxes (right and below right), the artist has unified the border and contents to produce a successful ensemble; a nice illustration of how framing materials may be selected for direct relevance to their contents. The glass fronts, which sit on top of the opening rather than in a rabbet, are simply clipped in place with brass clasps.

The variety of objects that can be framed is endless. Natural objects, such as shells, dried flowers, and even foodstuffs such as dried beans and nuts, are enormously popular, especially for display in kitchens and bathrooms. People often put together collections of personal items to create a framed piece to commemorate special occasions such as wedding anniversaries or a graduation. The challenge for the framer when presented with a commission of this sort is to find a way to group together disparate objects such as family snapshots, old concert programs, even small items of clothing like baby shoes. They need to be secured in place in such a way that the fixtures are invisible and there is no damage to the items themselves, which can be difficult when dealing with different materials such as paper, fabric, wood, and plastic. Most framers will use a variety of methods within the same frame, including water-soluble adhesive, photographic corners, sewing, and stapling. Of course, the primary concern is that the overall composition is attractive.

For a more flexible arrangement, the front of the frame could be hinged so that the contents are quickly and easily accessible. To do this, the outer frame molding should be constructed as a separate glazed unit; thin strips of wooden beading secured on the underside of the glass with glazing pins will hold the glass safely in place. Dividers inside the box itself, that form separate compartments, could replace the need for permanent fixtures. In a frame like this, it is possible to create a succession of ever-changing temporary arrangements, so this is an ideal way to display material which might not last very long, such as dried flowers which will fade over time, or mementos and memorabilia gathered on vacation. As an alternative to hanging them on a wall, these boxes can be displayed vertically on flat surfaces such as coffee tables, where their contents can be readily viewed.

The rustic simplicity of the painted wooden apples and pears in these two frames (below) is well served by the gentle cream-colored boxes in rough unfinished wood and the straightforward unadorned green frames.

A favorite pipe (above) is given exaggerated importance by the use of framing materials usually reserved for museum exhibits. A broad sweeping green baize covers the inner frame, and the outer frame is made of polished walnut veneer.

The neatly boxed compartments lend an air of order and formality to this delightful collections of nuts, acorns, seeds, and dried petals and leaves, simply and appropriately framed in lightly stained pine.

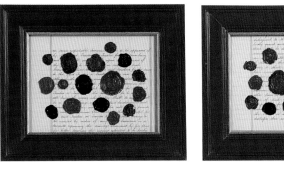

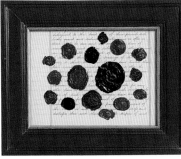

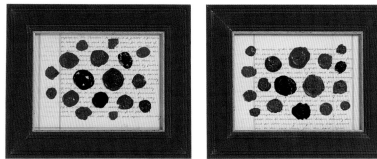

This is a dignified treatment for a collection of medals (above): symmetrically arranged in a simple polished wood display case, lined with blue and red velvet.

The background chosen for this collection of wax seals— pages cut from an old legal document—is both appropriate and attractive (top). The broad frame in red lacquer ties in with the color of the seals.

EPHEMERA AND COLLECTIONS

Ephemera as a category covers all those items whose original purpose was intended to be short-lived and which were expected to be discarded, such as postage stamps, labels, old-fashioned food packaging, and greeting cards. However many of these things, by their very nature, have a strong visual and graphic identity. They were originally designed to appeal, and it is this quality that makes them attractive to collectors and has saved many of them from their intended fate—obsolescence. This same decorative quality also makes them ideal candidates for framing.

Single items, such as individual greeting cards, can be treated in the same way as you would a frame a small watercolor or print. Collections tend to need more elaborate solutions, unless all the items are of exactly the same size, as with cigarette cards. It may be appropriate to arrange the pieces against, say, a fabric background set back within a plain mat border to give unity. Alternatively, an inner box divided into compartments, each containing an individual item, can produce an interestingly different way to present the collection so that it is seen as a whole, but each piece stands in its own right.

Two Victorian greeting cards are given differing but both very attractive treatments. For each, an appropriately colored marble paper has been selected for the background and the mat is covered in pretty silk. The delicately molded 19th-century gilt frame (right) and the fine copper-leaf frame (below) complete the decorative effect.

An assortment of ceramic buttons neatly arranged against a dark background (far right) is given importance by the broad reeded frame with its simple ivory colored finish.

Fans are normally framed individually in specially shaped fan cases, as in this example (right), finished in gold leaf; the molded plaster decoration of the frame echoes the ribbed spines of the fan itself.

THE
CRAFT
OF FRAMING

WHEN YOU STEP INTO A PICTURE FRAMER'S
STUDIO YOU ENTER A WORLD WHICH IN
CERTAIN KEY RESPECTS HAS CHANGED
REMARKABLY LITTLE FOR GENERATIONS.

Some of the principal types of
wood that framers work with:
clear pine and a flat molding
in paler ash (right) and
darker oak (opposite). These
are used in their natural state
or stained, lightly colored, or
polished. Smooth, almost
grainless obeche (opposite) is
used as a base for more
elaborate finishes.

THE SKILLS REQUIRED OF A GOOD framemaker are both practical and artistic. The tools and machinery employed have evolved so that now tasks which were formerly laborious and time-consuming can be completed in a fraction of the time. The materials used have also been developed to such a point that it is possible to achieve excellent results with factory-finished mat boards and moldings. But in essence the core tasks remain the same and are done mainly by hand; the framer cuts and joins lengths of wood, prepares a mat and cuts glass and board and assembles the component parts together to produce the completed frame. Beyond this a framer with experience and expertise will be undertaking a whole array of more complex tasks, employing skills that are little different from those used by the craftsmen depicted in the earliest engravings of framemakers' workshops.

Although sophisticated machinery now exists which means that mats can be bevel cut and moldings to be mitered and joined quickly and efficiently, practical expertise and manual dexterity are still essential in many areas. In particular, a certain amount of woodworking knowledge is needed for constructing more complex frames, for carrying out repairs to old frames, and for tackling specialized tasks such as carving or veneering. Experience in working with raw wood is also essential for understanding how different woods behave given different treatments—when finishing with stains, color washes, and polishes, for example.

Artistic skills and sensibilities come to the forefront in two particularly important areas. Of course, an eye for color, shape, and composition is a prerequisite for advising and deciding on how a particular painting should be framed in the first place. Then, a good framer will seek to do more than just rely solely on the mass-produced mat boards and moldings that are readily available. He will want to achieve a more individual result, in many cases by decorating the mat and finishing the frame by hand. The embellishment of mats with line and wash borders originated some three hundred years ago, and the methods by which they are produced, with colored inks and watercolors, have remained virtually unchanged since then. Finishes on frames have evolved with the development of new paints and varnishes that are faster-drying and more durable, but here again the same aesthetic skills are needed for producing the most rewarding results in the exact color and look achieved.

Both practical and artistic skills combine in the most timeless finish of all on frames—the application of sheets of pure gold leaf to cover moldings. The technique of water gilding originated in ancient Egypt and the process is still essentially the same, requiring patience and a steady hand.

MATS

Works on paper are normally mounted either by being placed against a backing board, where the deckled edge of a print is to be shown, for example, or displayed inside a window mat.

Both for presentation and for protection original works on paper are most often displayed inside a window mat, that is, a board with the central section cut out. The bevel cut of the window mat must be perfectly even and regular, and this is almost always achieved nowadays by means of a special mat-cutting machine.

Mat board is produced either in plain form, suitable for use as it is or for decoration by the framer, or surfaced with colored paper. The quality of the board varies enormously, from cheap board prepared with woodpulp, through board which has been treated to remove harmful chemicals (acid-free conservation board) to the best quality boards which are manufactured from pure rag only (museum board). Good framers prefer to use boards which are acid free, and they will also have the skills to achieve more individual effects by covering mats with fabric or a specialist paper, such as Ingres or Fabriano, or a handmade product, for example Japanese or Indian paper. The fabric or paper may be pasted, or "wet-mounted," onto the board, or affixed by a method known as dry mounting. This involves the use of an adhesive tissue which bonds when heated in a dry-mount press. For best effect the mat opening is cut first and the surface fabric or paper applied afterward and then wrapped around the bevel, as illustrated here.

CUTTING THE WINDOW

A mat-cutting machine is composed of a bar incorporating a sliding head which holds the cutting blade at a 45-degree angle; this creates a neat beveled edge. Adjustable stops guarantee the cut starts and finishes in exactly the right position.

COVERING THE MAT

A piece of red Japanese paper and a piece of dry-mount tissue are cut to the same size as the mat. Using a heated electric tacking iron, the framer secures the tissue to the front of the mat and to the decorative paper. Small pieces of plastic-backed paper prevent scorching. The covered mat is then placed in a hot dry-mount press to seal the paper.

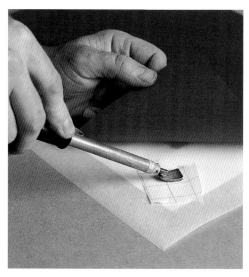

Once the mat is laminated, the paper in the center is cut away, leaving a narrow border to be wrapped over the bevel. The inner corners are mitered and the edges folded back through the window and tacked down at the back with the iron. The mat is placed in the press once more to be sealed on the underside.

CONSTRUCTING A DOUBLE MAT

Mats in contrasting colors can be combined to form a double, or stepped, mat. The framer applies strips of double-sided tape to the back of the mat with the larger window in preparation for a second mat to be attached.

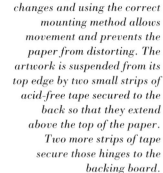

MOUNTING THE ARTWORK

Paper expands and contracts slightly with atmospheric changes and using the correct mounting method allows movement and prevents the paper from distorting. The artwork is suspended from its top edge by two small strips of acid-free tape secured to the back so that they extend above the top of the paper. Two more strips of tape secure those hinges to the backing board.

The red outer mat is positioned carefully over the inner mat, in this case cut from a board already surfaced in green paper, and pressed firmly to secure it. The window in the green mat is cut slightly smaller so that a narrow, even border of green is visible inside the red mat.

MAKING A HINGED MAT

A piece of backing board is hinged to the reverse side of the window mat using a strip of strong, usually linen, acid-free tape, to form a "book" or hinged mat. The artwork will be totally protected within this case.

The final result: a print of a macaw mounted in complementary colors of Japanese red and an inner mat in green.

MAT DECORATION

For the imaginative framer, the ability to produce a broad range of decorative mats is one of the most demanding, but above all rewarding, parts of the job.

It is an area in which technical skill and aesthetic judgment must come together to achieve the ideal result—both harmonizing with and enhancing the picture. One of the simplest means of embellishing the mat is to tint the bevel edge with watercolor paint; alternatively, the bevel can be wrapped in paper, a decorative device which can be used to good effect on the inner board of a double mat.

More often, decoration is applied to the mat surface, and for this the traditional method using watercolors is the most versatile and generally produces the most satisfying results. Line decoration is applied using a ruling pen, while a fuller effect is obtained with a washline border. The aim is to create in effect a subtle inner frame on the mat which corresponds to colors in the painting, ideally by high-lighting a subsidiary, rather than a dominant color in the watercolor or print. Strips of gummed gold or silver paper and borders of marbled or other sorts of decorative papers afford an additional device, for use alone with just a line of watercolor on each side or in conjunction with washlines.

As well as using watercolor to apply lines and washes the framer produces more varied effects with patterned fabrics or by applying strips of decorative paper.

DECORATIVE LINES

Having lightly marked the starting points of each line with a map pin and a calibrated plastic corner, the framer applies thin watercolor lines using a ruling pen and a metal straightedge as a guide. The adjustable nib on the pen allows for lines of varying thickness to be made. Watercolor lines can be used to decorate just the mat or as part of a washline border.

WASHLINES

For a traditional effect, a delicate color is applied with a watercolor brush in the center of an arrangement of four lines. More dramatic effects can be obtained by strengthening the color or by washing over the whole mat in watercolor or gouache using a broader brush.

LAYING A MARBLE STRIP

Gold or silver and marble papers are supplied in sheets that can be cut into strips as needed. A narrow gold paper border has already been applied to the mat shown here; a slightly wider marble paper strip is glued in place, using the watercolor lines as a guide.

COVERING THE BEVEL

Decorating the bevel edge of an inner mat is a very effective way of highlighting particular colors in the work being framed. Strips of gold paper are glued over the bevel, mitered at the corners and then turned over to the back of the mat and pressed in place with a burnisher.

MAKING THE FRAME

With machinery now available, the central task of the framer—cutting and joining the frame—has been rendered relatively simple and speedy.

The molding, which comes in lengths of up to 10 feet, either raw or ready-finished, is cut to size in a guillotine machine in which the blades are set to produce perfect mitered corners. Once cut, the sections are glued and joined. In the case of simpler jobs, involving a ready-finished molding, the frame is now complete and ready to assemble with its picture.

But the joining of the frame may be only the first step. Often the bare frame must be finished, and on the following pages some of the intricate processes involved are shown. Additionally, an inner frame, or slip, may be required— either gilt, painted, or covered in a fabric such as canvas, silk, or velvet. Frames for oils or acrylics often incorporate a slip to provide a narrow visual break between the painting and the frame. In addition to performing a visual function, a slip can also act as a practical device; thus, when glazing is needed to give protection, the slip is placed under the glass to create a gap. The same result may also be obtained, but with a neater effect, by constructing a simple box or shadow frame; in this case, the rabbet under the glass is lined with slivers of wood wide enough to give clearance to the items being framed, usually three-dimensional objects. The wood can then be finished in a manner appropriate to the frame, or to the mat, or both.

CUTTING THE MOLDING

A guillotine cutter with two blades set at right angles to each other cuts into the length of molding to form the four sections which will make up a complete frame. Normally the machine is set to produce 45-degree miter corners in each section, but it can be adjusted to cut different angles: to produce hexagonal frames, for example.

JOINING THE CORNERS

In general, framers now use a machine known as an underpinner to join the corners. The sections are glued and then clamped in the jaws of the machine. The joint is secured by "V"-shaped metal wedges, which are pushed in by the machine from underneath.

INSERTING A SLIP

The completed frame is hung up for the glue to set and is then ready for assembling with the painting—or with glass, backing board, and mounted work in the case of a print or watercolor. Here, however, the frame is intended for an oil painting and so an inner canvas-covered frame, the slip frame, is being secured in place.

THE EFFECT OF THE SLIP

The canvas slip frame sits inside the rabbet of the outer frame, and so forms a bridge between the painting and the frame.

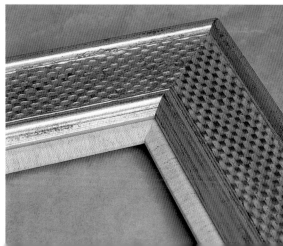

MAKING A BOX FRAME

To display three-dimensional objects, the depth of the frame must be much greater than usual. To make a box frame, the framer lines the inside of the frame rabbet with slivers of wood, which can be stained or painted to match the finish of the frame molding, or covered with paper as shown here.

LINING WITH FABRIC

For a particularly sumptuous effect, the inside of a box can be lined with fabric. To achieve a perfect result, without frayed edges or ugly seams in the fabric, each section of the frame is individually covered before being glued and joined. Here lengths of molding are covered with strips of velvet to form a slip.

FIXING THE OBJECT

The backing board is covered in the same fabric as the side sections, and the object to be displayed, here a medallion, is sewn in place. The back is then attached to the slip, or in this case deeper side sections, and the assembled velvet box is secured in place in the glazed outer frame.

COLOR WASH

The application of a wash of diluted paint lets the grain of the wood show through. With some color finishes such as white or off-white, the paint is left as it is, giving a chalky effect. But the finish may also be sealed with wax polish or flat or gloss varnish, all of which will deepen the color.

PICKLING

To achieve a pickled finish on woods such as oak or ash, white wax is rubbed into the grain. The wood is then cleaned with steel wool so that the wax residues are left in the grain only. Finally the surface is polished hard with a soft cloth to a shiny finish.

SIMPLE FRAME FINISHES

Few framers will be content to rely solely on ready-finished moldings; most find it far more rewarding, when the painting demands, to work up from the raw wood to create an individual finish.

Stains, color washes, and polishes, as well as combinations of all three, can all be applied to wood to deepen or change its natural color and finish. In certain instances, as with oak, some staining is often desirable if the grain of the wood is to be emphasized.

Alternatively, the raw wood frame may be treated with a color finish, either using a color stain or by applying coats of paint thinned with mineral spirits or with water, and mixed to a color appropriate for the picture; the paint method generally allows more versatility in achieving exactly the desired result. Thereafter, the color wash can either be left as it is, which lends a slightly chalky look to the frame where water-based paints are employed—particularly effective with white or off-white finishes—or it may be sealed in with wax polish. White wax polish can also be applied directly to the bare wood, which also produces a fake pickled effect.

A further stage is reached with solid color effects. As a general rule, it is rarely satisfactory to attempt finishes with a single color, but an enormous range of effects may be obtained by overlaying dramatically contrasting colors. Thus, for example, putting down a solid base in Etruscan or Chinese red, followed by a diluted coat of black, creates a rich, hot finish not unlike the look of antique rosewood. The same top coat on a base of yellow ocher produces an entirely different effect, akin to that of old dark-stained timber. More vibrant finishes may be achieved with base coats in strong blues, greens, and pinks washed over in contrasting colors.

WOODSTAINS

The cut sections of frame molding are stained before being joined, as the slight glue residues left at each corner during joining form a seal on the surface of the wood, which prevents the stain from going on evenly.

The stain raises the grain of the wood slightly, so steel wool is used to smooth the surface again before the application of beeswax polish.

COLOR ON COLOR

To produce a rich, interesting effect, two contrasting coats of solid color are used. In this case. an undercoat in a brown-red combination provides the base for a top coat in black, which is brushed on thinly.

When the top coat is dry, it is rubbed back with steel wool so that the reddish base reveals itself; vigorous wax polishing produces a warm glow in the finish.

DECORATIVE EFFECTS

There is no need to confine your choices to simply finished frames—a good framer can apply imagination and artistic endeavors to produce dramatic results.

When the painting or print, or even indeed the interior decoration of the room, suggests this course of action, the simple wood and paint finishes shown on the previous pages can be further elaborated by the use of more complicated techniques. This is potentially a vast field and, depending on the skills of the framer, a huge array of the traditional painter-decorator's techniques, as well as those of the fine artist, can be brought into play. For our purposes, however, we have chosen to confine ourselves to three or four approaches which provide a sound starting point from which to adventure further.

DRAGGING

One of the simplest techniques is known as dragging, in which a lighter base tone is revealed under a darker tone. When dragging walls and doors, decorators tend to use eggshell paint for the base coat and oil-based glazes for the top coat, but for frames where the surface area to be covered is so much less, and where speed of drying is often a priority, any water-based paint will do. Here, a first coat of pale blue has been allowed to dry thoroughly, and now a darker blue wash is being laid rapidly over the base color.

Working fast, before the darker wash has time to dry, a dry brush is drawn quickly along the lengths of the frame in one smooth movement. This exposes the underlying lighter blue and produces the dragged effect. This effect depends upon clean lines, so the bristles are dried by wiping off on a clean rag or some scrap paper between strokes. Different thicknesses of brush can be used for slightly different finishes.

COMBING

Similarly, in these examples of finished frames, the top layer of a darker wash has been drawn or scraped off, in this case using metal and rubber combs creating a more etched look. For different effects and different widths of pattern, teeth can be cut into pieces of stiff cardboard. A variety of different patterns, such as cross-hatching and wavy lines, can be experimented with using these methods.

STENCILING
AND PAINTED MOTIFS

Designs can be cut into a stiff nonabsorbent material such as waxed cardboard or, as in this case, transparent plastic film. The paint is stabbed through the design onto the frame using a stubby brush. Decorative designs painted freestyle can also enhance a frame, as in this classically inspired corner detail.

ELABORATE FRAME FINISHES

Simple techniques, used in combination with each other, can be used to create more sophisticated finishes, to make unusual and very luxurious frames.

Sponging, that is, using various small natural sponges to apply paint, is a very useful and versatile technique. Used by itself it provides a simple broken paint effect which can suit a variety of different situations. Used in conjunction with other methods, it can result in remarkably sophisticated finishes. Such finishes can be adapted to frames destined for a wide range of different images. Lapis lazuli is one of the richest and most luxurious of the paint finishes, particularly if completed by a gentle streaking or spattering of gold powder. The essence of this finish is to try to achieve something of the effect of the depth of color and tone that the different layers of veining in the stones naturally possess.

Using a variety of brushes and spattering tiny dots of color onto a sponged base coat can result in the very versatile porphyry finish. Natural porphyry comes in a variety of different tones, from green, through violet, gray, and brown, and most commonly a sort of maroon, all flecked with darker and lighter unevenly distributed dots which form a part of the stone itself. However, do not confine yourself only to naturally occurring colors, as this is a very useful and subtle finish to break up a solid color. It is not too intrusive in terms of pattern (which a strong marbled pattern can be) and is generally suitable for a whole range of situations—very much an interior decorator's favorite.

SPONGING

Very different finishes and effects can be achieved, depending on the size of sponge used and on its handling. This shows how a small pointed sponge used in a delicate jabbing motion creates a fine speckled effect. Two colors are being applied over a white base. The two finished frames have been given a similar treatment using different colors, and finished off with a coat of varnish.

A thicker sponge will give a more all-over covering effect. Two or more colors can be applied across the surface of the frame with more vigor. The trick here lies in juxtaposing the right colors or hues.

LAPIS LAZULI

There are different sorts of lapis lazuli, all of them with an intensity and depth of color that can make a marvelous decorative finish. A combination of sponged marks and brush strokes are built up over several layers to create the right effect. A dusting of gold powder is being flicked across the recently varnished and therefore still sticky frame surface. When it has dried, the excess powder will be blown away and a further coat of varnish applied to lock in the gold.

Different examples of porphyry, including a stylish frame combining gold leaf and a lightly spattered center section, show how versatile this finish can be.

PORPHYRY

Painting techniques can be used to imitate the effect of closely polished stone, such as granite. The effect is built up in stages. Here the base coats are a watery shade of pinkish brown sponged onto the light pink ground.

An old stencil brush is filled with the desired color and spattered randomly across the frame, varying the intensity of dots and marks. To create a true porphyry effect, several colors should be used for the spattering, including whites and very dark blues or blacks. Finish with a coat of varnish, a gentle rub with steel wool, and buff with beeswax polish.

TORTOISESHELL

A light, bright base coat is painted onto bare wood and sanded very smooth when dry. This can be bright orange, scarlet, or a very strong cadmium yellow. The darker tortoiseshell markings, comprising small tadpole shapes and longer swelling strokes, are then painted on diagonally, keeping the direction of the markings consistent with the illusion of veneered tortoiseshell.

The rather jazzy markings and bright undercoat are then subjected to a glutinous layer of shellac or button polish, applied with a soft varnish brush until the desired depth of tone has been achieved. The lighter finished frame has been prepared slightly differently, applying the blurring technique used in marbling, so that the diagonal marks seem to merge into one another.

SPECIALIZED FINISHES

Sometimes a print or a painting will call for a particularly stylized frame, and in those cases sumptuous fake natural finishes are an ideal choice.

A sober marble finish, for example, in conjunction with a suitable mat can look elegant and cool on an architectural print; while a powerful black-and-white print by the Italian artist Giovanni Battista Piranesi (*c.* 1720–78) could take a rich green serpentine marble effect. Having a small piece of polished marble by your side is a useful guide, though it is equally important not to be totally slavish; it is in the end only an illusion that you are striving to achieve.

Fake tortoiseshell is another finish that has numerous applications to the picture framer. Historically, both genuine tortoiseshell veneers and painted imitation tortoiseshell were frequently used in 16th- and 17th-century northern Europe. Today fake tortoiseshell is often used with decorative prints that are botanical in theme, for example, and in its cruder, more obviously painted form, it can be very effective with so-called naïve or primitive paintings or prints. Combined with polished black painted "ebony" corners, or raised outer and inner sections, it can be very elegant.

All these finishes can, of course, be combined with other techniques such as gilding, or even with one another.

MARBLING

The starting point is a white or light base coat, sanded to a smooth ivory finish. Then the main marble colors and tones are applied with sponges, brushes, and tissues. It may take some time and several layers to reach the desired intensity, but it is important at the same time to leave vestiges of the base tone showing through here and there.

The veins and fault-lines of the stone, in this case whites, near-blacks, and flashes of red, are then fidgeted in using a light flicking motion with a fine sable brush; a soft dry badger brush is kept handy to blur and shift some of these lines before they dry fully, in imitation of the different layers of the striations found in real marble. Again, the buildup of lines and blurrings is an essential part of the process.

To finish, a coat of flat varnish is applied. To recreate the soft sheen so typical of marble, the dry varnish is polished with steel wool, and then given a final polish with a beeswax preparation.

Two variations of a marble finish including (right) a brown fossilstone marble. The trick here is to drop discreet amounts of denatured alcohol or turpentine onto the water-based washes and to reduce or eliminate altogether the painted lines.

WATER GILDING

The gilder prepares a perfect surface using gesso, a plaster-like mix of chalk whiting, size, and water. The first, thin coat acts as a sealant; the next eight to twelve coats are thickened with extra whiting, and each coat is allowed to dry before the next is applied. Finally, the surface is rubbed with progressively finer grades of sandpaper until it is absolutely smooth.

Four to six coats of the clay-based bole are applied. The color of the bole influences the color of the final finish and also has just the right level of absorbency for the water gilding process. The dry bole is then meticulously smoothed, ultimately with fine steel wool, so there is no hint of unevenness.

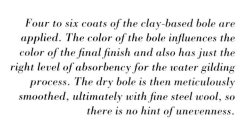

The fine wafers of real gold leaf disintegrate at the slightest disturbance. The gilder slides a leaf onto a gilder's cushion, where it is flattened out and cut to the required size. She brushes the gilder's tip against her face to create static and with it picks up a sliver of gold and places it onto a moistened area of the bole. She then gently presses the leaf into place using a squirrel-hair brush.

To make sure the leaf is pressed into the crevices of the molding, a burnishing tool tipped with agate is used. Agate is a soft, smooth stone which does not disturb the gold.

GILDED FRAMES

The application of pure gold leaf is demanding of skill, time, and patience, but its subtlety of color and depth of tone give a most rewarding finish.

Water gilding is the most difficult form of gilding to apply. So named because it is water that provides the initial means of applying the gold leaf, it is perhaps the most universally acceptable and applicable finish for frames. It provides the perfect abstract color with which to isolate the image from its surroundings, and it is equally suitable for oil paintings, watercolors, and prints.

There are considerable variations in the colors of gold leaf available, ranging from very pale lemony yellows to rich reddish golds. The final color is further affected by the color of the ground onto which the leaf is laid. This ground is made from bole, a clay containing iron oxides which comes in a variety of ochers, pinks, reds, blues, and black, and when the gold leaf is burnished, the tones of the bole show through. The bole will itself have been applied on top of several coats of plaster-like gesso fine enough to have filled in the slightest imperfections in the surface of the wood. Without this initial perfectly laid surface, the gold leaf will never look right.

Water gilding is the preferred option for the main surfaces of a frame, while oil gilding, which is technically easier to apply, might be used for more inaccessible carved

Gilding tools and equipment have remained virtually unchanged for centuries.

sections of a frame. Water-gilded surfaces can be dusted, but should never be wiped with a damp cloth, as the finish is water-soluble and remains relatively fragile. The crevices of a deeply carved frame can be cleaned using a soft-haired brush.

Apart from pure gold leaf, there are other types of metal leaf that can be applied to frames in much the same way as pure gold leaf. White gold, for example, is an alloy of gold and silver, and you can also get silver leaf and platinum leaf. Apart from the obvious color difference from traditional gold leaf, these metal leaf finishes differ in the way they behave over time. They will tarnish fairly quicky when exposed to the atmosphere and they therefore have to be protected in some way by a seal or a varnish. This in itself offers scope for further variations in the finished effect, since pigment can be added to the varnish. Sepia, for example, will impart a warmer, more aged glow to an otherwise silver frame. The tarnishing process itself can be used to good decorative effect; it can be allowed to progress a little way before being halted and sealed by the application of a protective film.

A cheaper alternative to real gold leaf is Dutch metal or "Schlag," which is a transfer leaf. In this process, instead of using water as with water-gilding, an oil size is brushed onto the bole and it is to this that the transfer leaf adheres. Again, this leaf will tarnish and therefore needs to be sealed.

Pure gold leaf does not need any kind of protective seal or varnish as it will not tarnish, but will retain its shine indefinitely. This shine is achieved using an agate stone burnisher. These burnishers come with a variety of different-shaped agates to deal with the different shapes of frame, some rounded, some pointed, and so on. Once burnished, the job may be completed, but in certain instances it is desirable to embark on the final stage known as distressing. Using cotton balls and fine steel wool this can range from simply knocking back a very shiny, over-brash gold-leaf finish, perhaps unsuitable for a painting with subdued colors, to abrading the gold leaf in such a way as to reveal quite considerable amounts of the underlying bole, achieving more of an antique effect. After the considerable time and patience put into gilding a frame, the skill in distressing lies in knowing exactly at what point to stop.

SILVER GILT FRAMES

Silver leaf and white gold leaf, an alloy of gold and silver, both tarnish with exposure to the air and must be sealed. The sealant may be clear, or tinted to produce an aged effect.

BURNISHING

Gold leaf has a dull appearance when first applied; to bring it up to a rich effect, it has to be rubbed with an agate stone burnisher.

DISTRESSING

Lightly rubbing the burnished surface of the gilt with cotton balls or fine grade steel wool removes some of the gold leaf to reveal traces of the colored bole beneath.

CRAQUELURE OR CRACKED GESSO FINISHES

The prepared strips of cracked gesso are glued down to the bare wood frame and then clamped in place until they have dried.

Light washes of thin color can be applied to either cracked or smooth gesso finishes, or the gesso can be toned for an ivory-look finish.

The full effect of the hairline cracking can be seen on this shallow reverse frame, which has had cracked gesso applied to the center section, between gold-leaf inner and outer edges.

APPLIED FINISHES

As an alternative to painting or gilding, frames may be finished using techniques of applied decoration, such as veneering and craquelure, traditionally used in cabinet making and interior decoration.

Veneers are extremely thin sheets of fine woods, such as walnut, maple, mahogany, ebony, and rosewood, which are glued to the surface of a frame made out of a cheaper wood. In the past, tortoiseshell and ivory were applied in the same way. Wood veneers are nowadays machine-cut from the lumber into sheets ⅟₁₆ inch thick and then glued and clamped until set. When the veneer is solidly attached it is smoothed down, and the color heightened with stain if required, and then it is sealed or polished to a rich finish.

Another important applied finish involves the use of craquelure or cracked gesso. This finish was popularized by the English decorator Syrie Maugham in the 1920s and was applied to furniture, boxes, and so on, but it has survived most successfully in picture-framing. Coats of gesso are applied to fabric which, when dry, is rolled, producing fine cracks in the surface of the plaster. The fabric is then cut into thin strips ready to be applied to the frame.

VENEERED FRAMES

Walnut and maple are the most frequently used veneers. Flat or turned ebony wood corners decorate some of the light veneer frames, while others have marquetry decoration, formed by inserting small pieces of veneer in a contrasting color to form patterns within the main veneer. Smaller sections can also be cut and glued across the width of the frame, a variation known as crossbanding.

Re-gluing and nailing loose corners is usually a straightforward task. But if the wood has shrunk, the framer may separate and recut the corners, provided there is no plaster molding to be disturbed.

To replace missing pieces of decoration, the framer will first select an intact section of frame that is an exact match for the damaged area. Flexible soft clay pressed into the frame forms a mold.

RENOVATING A FRAME

The surprising increase in the value of antique frames in recent years has made it worthwhile restoring those that have been damaged.

Frequently old frames have deteriorated over time—the corners have come loose, the plaster decoration has been knocked off, and the gold surface scuffed or rubbed away. All of these faults can be repaired. Another problem which arises with antique frames is that they have been overpainted at some point with cheap gold paint. The taste in the 19th century was for very bright gilding, and as frames faded, the owners would apply a coat of metallic gold paint to freshen them up. These paints tarnish to an unattractive bronze color. Hasty amateur attempts to remove this layer can easily result in the original finish and even the gesso being removed as well. But an expert restorer will first test to see whether there is any original gilding, then carefully remove the offending paint and restore the old finish.

Quick-drying repair paste is pressed into the mold and left to set hard.

When the flexible clay mold is pulled away (left), the new cast is revealed in hardened repair paste.

A good repair will be invisible, indistinguishable from the rest of the undamaged molding (right). Burnishing and then distressing with cotton balls (below right) complete the finish so the repaired areas match the original.

To achieve an exact fit, the framer sands the edges of the newly cast piece until it slots perfectly into the damaged section. Only then is it glued into place.

When the glue is dry, the framer must then finish the plaster cast to match the rest of the frame. Several coats of gesso provide a smooth base coat and disguise the seams. Bole is applied next, before finishing with gold leaf.

HANGING
AND
DISPLAY

HOW PICTURES ARE ARRANGED IS OF
PARAMOUNT IMPORTANCE, EQUAL TO THE
CHOICE OF THE FRAME. WHATEVER CARE
AND THOUGHT HAS BEEN GIVEN TO ITS
FRAMING, A PICTURE WILL ONLY COME
INTO ITS OWN ONCE IT IS DISPLAYED.

The careful planning of this group of three drawings in fine gilt and black frames allows them to be seen to good advantage (right), but conforms to the clear-cut elegant look of the room with its light wood furniture and pale walls.

The traditional method of hanging paintings, from brass hooks on a picture rail, continues to be a simple and practical alternative to hooks driven into the wall. Pictures can then be moved easily and the walls are left unmarked, although the method is only really suitable for hanging a single row.

IN A SENSE THE FRAMING PROCESS is complete only when the painting has taken its place on the wall. Hanging pictures successfully presents a two-fold challenge. The pictures, whether individually or, if in a set or a series, as a group, must themselves be seen at their best advantage. In addition, though, pictures play such a vital role in interior decoration that the decision on how each is placed will crucially affect the character of the room. This section will look at the ways in which the enjoyable and rewarding task of arranging your pictures should be approached, both in general terms, and by focusing on particular hanging plans and on specific areas that may present problems.

Although the all-important decisions on hanging are aesthetic there are some practical aspects to be considered at the outset. The first of these concerns the method of hanging. Good framers will normally provide hardware on the frame, and cord or wire of adequate strength to take the weight of the picture. It is worth insisting on this; the framer is better placed than you to know what is needed. Next, decide on the appropriate hanging system for your wall. For most purposes a standard picture hook driven firmly into the wall provides enough support, although particularly hard walls will need hooks with three or four pins specially made for this purpose. On a plaster wall that is soft or crumbly it may be better to drill through to the brick behind and put in a screw embedded in an anchor or use a long wall bolt. Use two hooks spaced apart if the picture weighs more than 15 pounds or is more than 3 feet long. Anything which weighs over 30 pounds—oil paintings in heavy old gilt frames or large mirrors, for example—should on no

account be hung using the normal wire or cord. The safe method is to use picture chain and to position screws in the wall on each side of the picture so that it can be suspended using two separate lengths of chain, thus spreading the weight evenly.

The other initial concern when considering the positioning of pictures is the light levels in the room. Certain paintings, watercolors in particular, will deteriorate if exposed to strong light so it is preferable to position them in an area which is away from direct sunlight. In addition, the reflection from large windows can prove to be an irritating distraction from the image on glazed works. Pictures also suffer from the effects of heat and, in particular, should not be placed immediately above uncovered radiators. Whereever possible the radiator should be covered with a shelf or casing to deflect the heat away.

White walls and a spare, uncluttered interior combine to give maximum prominence to the pictures and sculptures displayed.

A selection of fashion prints, unified by the framing and grouped informally within the context of a highly decorative interior, produce an effect of calm and luxury. The prints are linked to the decorative style of the room by the fabric hanging cords and rosettes.

FIRST
PRINCIPLES

Pictures establish the look and mood of a room as much as the colors and furniture, so at the outset it is worth devoting some thought to the effect you wish to achieve. The pattern in which the pictures are arranged; the use of space; juxtaposition with furniture; the different effects, or absence, of color: all these factors exert a powerful influence on the overall character of a room. Consider whether you want to establish a look that feels calm or busy, cool or warm, spare or luxurious. Alternatively, your aim might be to strike a balance with a bold and dramatic statement on one wall, softened by an informal group in another area of the room.

On a practical level, the best way to make a start is quite simply to stand pictures around the room and shuffle them around trying out different combinations. By seeing how paintings look against other paintings, how they appear in

relation to fabric colors and furniture, and how they fit into the various spaces available, you will be able to develop your ideas both as to the general look of the room and the ideal way to show particular works off to best advantage.

Where the pictures differ markedly in size, it makes sense to concentrate on the biggest and use this as a starting point. A large painting exerts a more pronounced influence on how the room is going to look and it may be that there are only a limited number of positions in which it can hang. Once it is in place, it will help to determine where the other pictures should hang. On the other hand, there may be a particular space, such as a chimney or the area over a sofa or a bed, which is a natural focus in a room; marrying this space with the right painting or group of pictures is important and should be dealt with at the outset. The other key spaces to concentrate on are the architectural areas that constitute minor focus points in a room, such as alcoves, and the narrow spaces beside windows, doors, and so on. Choosing something special for these places or utilizing them to assemble an interesting group often produces an effect beyond what you might expect.

An altogether different approach is to collect together pictures that form a coherent group and concentrate them in one room or on a single wall. Decorative prints, especially if they are united by a single theme, and works in different media but on the same subject (topographical views perhaps)

Defined spaces above particular items of furniture provide good focus points for the display of favorite paintings (above). The simple dignified arrangement of pewter pitchers and candlesticks on this marble-topped sideboard leads the viewer's eye up to the two landscapes.

This collection of differently shaped and framed works (above left) is brought together in an arrangement on a staircase wall which remains loose enough to be altered by additions or substitutions.

are good examples. Equally, collections of oil paintings or of drawings would be suitable; historically, the print room provided a model for this, with black-and-white engravings formally arranged. This hanging method stamps a room with a positive identity; oil paintings create a mood of gravity, drawings an academic look, costume prints a more luxurious feel, and modern photographs a cooler, spare impression.

The room size and, as important, height will influence your choice of suitable pictures and the way in which they are arranged. A low-ceilinged cabin is not going to be the ideal place for the massive equestrian portrait of one of your ancestors; equally, small paintings, needlework, and the like will be lost in a large space and should be sensitively placed in a more intimate setting, above a small item of furniture or in another clearly defined space.

Once you have decided what is going to go where, the next step is to consider the pattern of hanging. At one extreme is the formal arrangement, with each item carefully positioned to produce a regular display. This approach can achieve a calm and dignified effect, but it suffers the disadvantage of being inflexible; it is ideal for a finite set of prints, but restricting if you want to add to the original group. More haphazard arrangements, in contrast, produce an impression of comforting informality and can be altered at will. If you add to your collection of pictures from time to time, one of the rewards is the element of surprise which comes from re-hanging what you already possess; a new position and different lighting will often lead you to see a familiar painting with a new eye.

The height at which pictures are placed should also be considered. In halls, it is preferable for pictures to be positioned at eye level or slightly above; this allows them to be seen easily and means they are not brushed against in passing. In living rooms and bedrooms a lower hanging level is possible, especially where pictures are to be hung in more than one row. Bear in mind that when pictures are placed high up on the walls of a room they produce an austere look whereas arrangements starting at a lower level create a look that is more familiar and comfortable. Finally, you should consider the influence of light, both natural and artificial. Different types and sources of light alter the way you see pictures and it takes experimentation to arrive at the right placing for a particular painting or, with artificial light, the position of the light source. With oil paintings, especially traditional works executed in darker colors, the standard picture light will often be best.

A decorative ensemble is created by a grouping in which the picture is accorded equal status with the objects placed around it (above).

The shape of the frames is important here (left). The long print over the door, filling an otherwise unused space and making the doorway seem smaller, creates a feeling of intimacy in the room.

Propping pictures is a good short-term way to judge their overall effect in a room (below).

Paintings can be given enhanced effect by being placed close to furniture which highlights their colors (bottom).

The wall area above a couch is frequently a focus point in a room. This pair of minimally framed works (right) combine to create a single image, cool and unequivocally modern above the pale couch and table.

SMALL GROUPS

Assembling works in twos or threes can often be an easy and satisfying way to deal with a small areas such as an alcove or the space above a special item of furniture. Matching pairs and trios hang logically together, so identifying the right space to display them is a priority. But bringing together two or three pictures similar in size, in visual weight, or in subject matter offers a useful way to create interesting small-scale arrangements. And instead of placing a matching pair right next to each other, try separating them by inserting a differently shaped picture in between; ovals and other unusual frames work especially well in this format.

Creating interesting and coherent groups with pictures which differ in size and subject matter presents more of a challenge. Start by laying them out on the floor and moving them around to achieve a balance of size, color, and weight. The largest work in the group can provide an anchor. It may also help to visualize imaginary lines on the wall as a basis: a central horizontal line with pictures arranged above and below it or two or three vertical lines providing centers for column arrangements. These lines can be respected or trespassed upon, according to whether you want the end result to be formal or to give a more casual look. But the aim with these small groupings is always to make it appear that all the pictures go naturally together.

The asymmetrical arrangements in the two alcoves and the pictures casually placed against the fireplace introduce an air of informality (above).

The manner in which groups are arranged influences the mood of a room: this group (above left) avoids rigid symmetry, vertical or horizontal, and the effect is informal but coherent.

A pretty juxtaposition of a horizontal and a vertical grouping frame a bed (left).

This carefully
constructed group
(left) deftly combines
differently shaped
and framed pictures,
the prime focus being
the portrait in a
Louis XVI frame.

An asymmetrically
placed column acts as
a counterpoint to a
single picture (above).

The large painting
provides an anchor
that pulls together the
column arrangements
on each side (top).

A dramatic block of prints in primary colors dominates this very modern setting (far left). The frames echo the pale wood of the table.

The rectangular layout of these prints (left), homogeneous in subject matter and framing, is modified by the triangular pattern of the hanging system.

A row of small-scale pictures arranged in a row forms a graphic strip across the wall (below).

This block of pictures takes up the whole wall (below right). Their purpose is essentially decorative, in harmony with the furnishings.

REGIMENTED GROUPS

Hanging sets of pictures, or pictures which have been framed identically, in a regular formalized display will sometimes be the simplest and the most satisfying way to arrange them. The decision to follow this route may of course be taken for you if you have a number of paintings or prints by the same artist which should logically be placed together. Where a number of works have been executed on the same size canvas or paper with the intention that they be viewed as a whole, careful arrangement in a regimented block or sequence will probably be essential. The choice then is whether to hang the pictures in a straight line or in a block, arranged laterally or vertically, or in the form of a square. Room and wall size will affect your choice, but the works themselves may direct you to the ideal layout.

The choice of a regular format may be dictated by the interior decoration. Regimented groups of pictures can create a feeling of calm or introduce a note of order in a room where other elements are haphazard. Alternatively, a block of identically shaped and framed pictures may in itself be powerful enough to provide the focus to one area of the whole room. Achieving a formal arrangement entails care and precision, of course—careful measurement is essential to make sure the whole arrangement stays in line.

THE COLLECTOR

The collector's approach to picture hanging is driven more by interest in the pictures for themselves than by a desire to achieve decorative effects in the home. This creates an altogether different look in which the natural unhurried growth of an eclectic collection is reflected in the manner in which it is arranged. In these arrangements the pictures themselves are the prime focus, taking precedence over careful notions of interior decor.

More often the layout is informal, not least because collectors periodically shift paintings around as they acquire more or as their taste develops and changes. Since there are periodic additions to be accommodated, displays tend to be massed, haphazard, and asymmetrical, though order can be introduced by sticking to column formats or hanging by reference to notional horizontal lines, and in particular by aligning the tops of the pictures and arranging from there downward. One guideline to be kept in mind with mass displays of this sort is that, in a mix of large and small works, the larger pictures and bolder images should be placed higher and works with finer detail placed at a lower level where they can be easily appreciated.

In organic collections of this sort, different subjects and media are usually mixed, though attention has to be paid to balancing the visual weight of adjacent pictures. This may

A classic collector's arrangement on a staircase brings together a number of works of different medium and subject matter (above).

This display has been extended out onto a large easel (far left), creating an eccentric effect and demanding the viewer's attention.

Starting with a level top line a more ordered display can be achieved (left).

The formality of a room can be modified by quirky placement of a disparate collection (below).

A collection can almost fill a room, leaving no space between the pictures (bottom).

Mass arrangements will often be haphazard, incorporating pictures in widely differing sizes and allowing scope for additions (right).

preclude large acrylics and oil paintings as being too overwhelming—they would dominate a group to the detriment of the other works—but smaller paintings, drawings, watercolors, pastels, prints, and in some cases photographs can be grouped together. In these displays the interest lies in the narrative offered by the content of the pictures, their proximity to one another, and what they have to say about their owner.

Variety can be brought to your picture arranging if you take a cue from this approach and select a room or particular area such as a staircase wall to try it out. Put together a selection of your favorite pictures and, as a shortcut, try different arrangements on the floor first. Creating the effect does not require the advice of a professional decorator, though juxtaposing works which differ in size, medium, and subject matter involves experimentation and takes time and patience to pull it off. The end result, however, will provide an interesting contrast to more formal arrangements you may have in other parts of the house.

HANGING A
SINGLE PICTURE

The relationship between picture, frame, and setting is never more important than when you are hanging a solo picture. Dealing with a group is far less daunting. If the art work itself is sensational, it can be married with confident framing and put in a prominent position to make a dramatic statement and set the tone for the whole room. The average-sized, conservative painting is more difficult. It needs to make a decorative contribution, but not be overstated. Better then to treat such subjects as an integral part of the room's overall style. It will help if the color and style of mat and frame provide a decorative link with other elements in the room, such as the furniture or the walls. And it may be that if you look at the architectural framework of the room, there will be areas which could provide an outer frame for the picture, such as the area between two windows, a chimney, or a recess.

The frame mirrors the proportions of the fireplace exactly, the gold frame relates to the brass accessories below, and a cream slip has been inserted which refers to the day bed. Combined with the quiet subject and tones of the drawing, the whole effect is one of calm order.

Andy Warhol's giant silkscreen print provides the only color in a black, white, and chrome interior, making a compelling image in the double-story room. Its contemporary style works with the furniture, yet a touch of formality is introduced by the old-fashioned window panes, echoed in the panels of the print. The picture is mounted in an acrylic sheet box frame.

A three-quarter length portrait always makes an imposing statement, and the effect is heightened when it is hung alone on a pale background. A gilt frame, deeply burnished to a mellow color, is the perfect complement to the shadowy shades of the painting.

The interior is relentlessly monochrome with clinical lines. The simply framed photographs, forming a single visual unit, continue the black-and-white linear theme but introduce movement and curves which relieve the severity of the room.

A pleasing period effect is produced by placing miniatures against a 19th century-style fabric embroidered in a floral pattern (left).

The predominantly black and gray tones of this group of pictures moderates the warm orange ocher of the wall behind (far left).

DIFFERENT BACKGROUNDS

More than any other single factor, the walls will set the feel of a room, with their dominant texture and pattern. But the most important determinant of mood is usually color. At one extreme, pure white walls will create a feeling of space and simplicity. At the other, deep colors will help to establish a particular ambience according to hue.

The pictures you select to put in a room, their framing style, and the manner in which they are hung will affect the initial mood, either modifying or confirming it. With dark backgrounds, traditional oil paintings and other works without mats will tend to merge, intensifying the effect, but you can opt instead to moderate the mood of the room by hanging pictures with generous pale mounts, such as black-and-white engravings. In general, pale or mid-color walls will provide an ideal background for watercolors and for most modern works, allowing the pictures themselves to create an atmosphere in the room.

Texture will moderate the effect of color so, for example brick, bare or painted, creates a more simple rustic look, while fabric coverings create an impression of enveloping luxury. This can itself impose limitations; fabric walls are

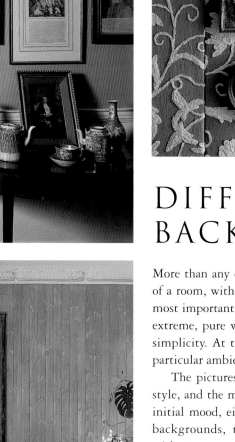

Avoiding strong contrasts, this arrangement places a painting against a background which is similar in feel, producing, with the couch below, a quietly comfortable overall effect (right).

more likely to suit delicate or decorative pictures. Bare brick can limit you, too—to robust oils paintings, primitive works, and perhaps framed objects—but, if it is painted, brick provides a more versatile and sympathetic background. Careful thought needs to be given to wood-paneled rooms. Paintings with warm, rich colors sit well against light paneling, but more of a challenge is posed by darker woods. Here you should decide whether to go with the somber feel by hanging pictures in deep tones or to bring light into the room, using pictures with generous pale mats. It may be better to avoid frames in wood which merge with the paneling and opt for a contrast; gold frames to hang against dark oak, colored frames against pine.

Patterned wallpapers offer different challenges and opportunities, although if the pattern is discreet, the color of the paper will be the deciding factor. Boldly patterned papers call for strong images in positive frames. In particular it may be necessary to use wide mats or frames to isolate the pictures from the background. The alternative is to use the pattern to create a luxurious effect by massing pictures against it or choosing works with elaborate frames.

The blue checks of the wallcovering produce a challenge, but a good solution has been found: isolating the two pictures by the use of broad wood veneer frames (above).

Sometimes bold combinations pay off, as with this vibrant painting of flowers. The violet blue of the wall offers a sensational background to the yellow and pink of the pictures and the strong black and gilt frame (left).

This painting in a wood veneer frame (left) combines harmoniously with the seat below.

Built-in bookcases (below) provide an excellent opportunity for showing pictures in a different manner.

A small painting displayed on an easel takes its place as an object when arranged with other pieces (bottom).

COMBINING
WITH OBJECTS

Arranging pictures with furniture is a familiar device, allowing interesting or harmonious connections to be made. At its simplest, this may consist in hanging pictures in wood veneer frames over a desk or an antique chest of drawers, or botanical subjects over a sofa covered in a floral pattern. Frames in decorative finishes such as fake marble can be particularly useful in this respect.

An equally fruitful area to explore is to combine pictures with objects, whether functional or ornamental, or with three-dimensional artwork, especially sculpture. To do this successfully with ornaments, some connection should be made, perhaps by color, pattern, or subject matter. Thus, oriental prints might be married with a Chinese vase, and black-and-white architectural subjects with ornaments that are monochrome, gray, or white. Try experimenting with different assortments of objects, bearing in mind that the aim is to create a harmonious group in which no one item is so dominant that it upsets the overall balance. Combining paintings with sculpture requires a different approach. As a work of art, a piece of sculpture needs to be given its own space, so it may be better to position it at a slight distance and avoid a crowded grouping, though connections can still be made through shape and color.

The key touch in this arrangement of a block of four architectural prints (left) is the link between the subject matter and the choice of adjacent objects. The glass obelisk echoes the stone obelisk in the top right-hand print.

Interesting combinations may be achieved by placing traditional pictures with modern sculpture (above). Both items inhabit distinct spaces but a subtle link is created between the black of the sculpture and the gray of the print.

A monochrome print provides a harmonious background for this display of objects on a geometric wrought-iron side table (right).

A steel structure in a rough concrete walled stairwell is successfully transformed by the large strong painting, and the carefully placed objects (left).

An odd corner is enlivened by three bright prints, profiting from the light streaming through the window, and by the colorful combination of a painting and a pitcher (right).

Instead of ignoring narrow corridors (below) it is worth enlivening these areas with something bold and eye catching.

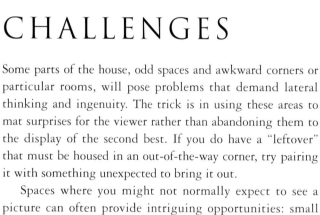

CHALLENGES

Some parts of the house, odd spaces and awkward corners or particular rooms, will pose problems that demand lateral thinking and ingenuity. The trick is in using these areas to mat surprises for the viewer rather than abandoning them to the display of the second best. If you do have a "leftover" that must be housed in an out-of-the-way corner, try pairing it with something unexpected to bring it out.

Spaces where you might not normally expect to see a picture can often provide intriguing opportunities: small bathrooms and foyers for example, the space above a doorway or under an eave, the turn on a confined staircase, a cupboard door. If you have a particularly unusual or quirky painting that refuses to sit comfortably alongside your other pictures, one of these spaces will often provide an ideal position. Framed objects are also a good choice; try placing fan cases above doorways and long vertical needleworks in narrow spaces beside windows.

Certain rooms present more practical problems, especially bathrooms and kitchens. The heat and in particular the steam in these rooms can do serious damage to delicate works, so hang reproductions and low-value prints in preference to watercolors or pastels. Different practical difficulties arise with eaved rooms and attic conversions. The spaces for hanging pictures will be restricted and oddly shaped, but in fact these truncated wall areas will afford added interest to anything which is placed on them.

The restricted space in an attic bedroom (top) has been put to interesting use by crowding together different-sized prints.

These shutters are usually kept closed (above) so the device of a removable brass hanging rod has been used both to secure them and to support the central row of pictures.

The juxtaposition of blue-and-white bowls with the picture against a strong blue wall distracts the eye away from a radiator (above).

Loft apartments present opportunities as well as challenges, and with careful thought and imagination, the unusual and irregular wall spaces can be turned to good use (right).

CREDITS

All illustrations are by Caroline McAdam Clark.

Key: *r* = right *l* = left *t* = top *b* = bottom *c* = center

The authors and publishers would like to thank the following people for loaning frames and framed artworks for inclusion in this book, and the artists for giving permission for their work to be shown. Every effort has been made to contact copyight owners where possible.

3 Trowbridge Gallery; 5 *bl* Stewart Heslop 8 *l* Stewart Heslop; 10 Wilkins & Wilkins; 13 *t* Stewart Heslop; 20–21 all frames Lacy Gallery; 23 *tr* Wilkins & Wilkins; 24–25 all frames Lacy Gallery; 26–27 all individual frames except *br* Wilkins & Wilkins; 28–29 all frames Lacy Gallery; 34 top row Rupert Cavendish Antiques; 34 *br* Wilkins & Wilkins; 37 *bl* Wilkins & Wilkins; 39 York Whiting; 41 *br* Lacy Gallery; 42–43 all frames Lacy Gallery; 44 *The Guitarist* by Laetitia Yhap; 45 *bl* Lacy Gallery; 51 restoration work carried out by Michael Cunningham and Alison Thomas; 55 *t Garden of Delights* by Caroline McAdam Clark; 55 *r Palazzo Dario* by Caroline McAdam Clark; 56 *Staircase, Menton* by Guy Roddon; 57 *Kohl-rabi* by Dennis Gilbert; 58 *tl Stellar* by Berthe Dubail; 58 *r* untitled by Caroline Feetham; 59 *t Fulham Power Station 1* by Sophie Macpherson; 59 *b The Birth of Mani* © 1997 Kim Poor (Billy Budis/Gallery K); 60 *l Still Life with Vase of Flowers* by John McCorquodale; 60 *t Bouziès, France* by Robert Organ; 61 *t* untitled by Caroline Feetham; 60 *r Party Girl with Black Velvet Choker* by Janet Patterson; 62 *Paul Cleaning a Cuttlefish* by Laetitia Yhap; 63 *Greek Landscape with Goat 1989* by Caroline McAdam Clark; 64 *A Foxhound* by John McCorquodale; 65 *t Portrait of Dr Arthur Melville Clark* by Adam Bruce Thomson OBE, RSA, PRSW; 65 *b A Pig by its Sty* by Michael Lynch; 66 conservation work carried out by Deborah Bates Conservation; 69 *tr* Laurelie Walter Interiors; 69 *b Pineapple Jug* by Geraldine Girvan (Chris Beetles Gallery); 70 *On the Beach* by Mary Adshead; 71 *l L'Anse aux Epines* by Stephen Bartlett *tr Cowpers Cross, 1995* by Simon Brown *b Boatyard II* by Alistair Grant (all Business Art Gallery); 72–73 *Venice, A Gondolier* by Stan Smith; 74 *l Brasserie Lipp, Paris* by Guy Roddon; 74 *r The Bathers* by Leon Ernest Drivier © DACS 1997; 75 *Still Life with Figs* by Rachel Hemming Bray; 77 gold frame Lacy Gallery; 78 *t Salome and Hare* by Linda Sutton; 78 *bl Paddy's Hole* by Graham Crowley; 78 *br Nude* by Larraine Lacey; 80 *l Testing Corn Plasters in the Salon of a Fashionable West End Chiropodist* by William Heath Robinson (Chris Beetles Gallery); 81 *t The 'Potter about the Hall all Day and Watch the Funny People Come and Go' Person* © estate of H.M. Bateman; 81 *br Red Ribbon* by Annie Tempest (O'Shea Gallery); 82 Pigeonhole Gallery; 83 A design for *Devil's Holiday* by Eugene Berman (Marina Henderson Gallery); 86 *l Kitty Levant les Bras et Adèle préparant le Bain 1902* by Suzanne Valadon © ADAGP, Paris and DACS, London 1997; 86 *r* Untitled lithograph – two women and a dog by Marie Laurencin © ADAGP, Paris and DACS, London 1997; 87 *tl Travnik, Bosnia* by Bernard Rice; 87 *tr* Untitled lithograph – female nude study by Aristide Maillol © ADAGP, Paris and DACS, London 1997; 87 *b Into the Night* by Samira Abbassy; 88 *t* and *r* Pigeonhole Gallery; 88 *l* O'Shea Gallery; 89 *r* O'Shea Gallery; 90–91 all Pigeonhole Gallery; 92–93 all O'Shea Gallery; 94 O'Shea Gallery; 95 *t* O'Shea Gallery; 95 *bl* Pigeonhole Gallery; 95 *br* O'Shea Gallery; 96 *l* Pigeonhole Gallery; 96 *c* and *r* Trowbridge Gallery; 97 all Pigeonhole Gallery; 100 *l Pink Collage 1978* by Caroline McAdam Clark; 100 *r* Wine collage by LoCole; 101 *l* Collage by Stephen Andrews; 101 *r Green and Yellow Collage 1978* by Caroline McAdam Clark; 103 *tr* O'Shea Gallery; 104 *tl Christ Chasing the Money Changers from the Temple* by Eric Gill; 104 *bl Portrait of a Boy 1989* by Caroline McAdam Clark; 106 *tr* Laurelie Walter Interiors; 107 *r* mounted series of original family photographs collected by Manuela Höfer; 108 *t Rose* by Bruce Rae; 108 *bl* original photographic print, colour toned, by Manuela Höfer; 108 *r* original photographic prints by Manuela Höfer; 109 both photographs by Jonathan Lovekin; 112 *l* produced by Sean Ford, framed by The Frame Factory; 112 *r* Shaker; 113 produced by Sean Ford, framed by The Frame Factory; 114 produced by Sean Ford, framed by The Frame Factory; 115 *Lapis* by Peter Cross (Lapis); 116 *l* produced by Sean Ford, framed by The Frame Factory; 116 *tr* produced by Sean Ford, metal box frame from Paperchase; 116 *br The Art Clock* by Joan Molloy (Lapis); 117 *l Astrantia* by Helen Smythe; 117 *r Female Figure Standing* by Sophie McCarthy; 118 three-dimensional collage and photo illustrations by Mandy Pritty; 119 *tl* The Pier; 121 *tr Porcelain Flowers* by Helen Smythe; 121 *br* Marina Henderson Gallery; 144 *b* Stewart Heslop; 148–49 Chain, rope and ribbon Laurelie Walter Interiors; 165 *l Still Life with Pink Vase* by Craigie Aitchison (Wiseman Originals); 170 Rupert Cavendish Antiques; 171 Simeon Smythe; 172 *Fishguard* by Lesley Donald (Framing Machine); 174 *Winter* by Helen Smythe; 175 photograph by Jonathan Lovekin; 176 Wilkins & Wilkins.

SOURCES

The following list includes framers and framemakers (F), who make and/or sell ready- and custom-made frames; restorers (R), who return frames to their original appearance; conservators (C), who reverse damage to frames and /or the paper or canvas the artwork is on; antique frame dealers (A), who restore and sell old frames; and art galleries (G), that provide framing as a service to their customers.

* Available only through architects and interior designers.

Absolute! Framemakers   (F R A)
8927 Ellis Avenue
Los Angeles, CA 90034
310-287-0700
Custom- and ready-made frames.

* Artistic Painting & Restoration (F R C)
2619 England Street
Huntington Beach, CA 92648
714-646-2007
Icon fabrication and restoration. Molding and carving.

Atelier Framing, Inc.   (F R C)
P.O. Box 7557
Portland, ME 04112
207-929-8822
Restoration of gilded frames. Custom-made new gilded frames.

* James K. Barter   (F R A)
RD 1, Box 292A
Franklin, ME
207-565-2279
Send photos for consultation

Beaucoup Framing & Gold Leaf Gallery   (F R G)
111 South Grand, Suite 108
Bozeman, MT 59715
406-585-8881
Custom framing and gilding.

Eugene Boemer   (F R C)
51 Tiffany Drive
Rehoboth Beach, DE 19971
302-645-9743
Reverse painting on glass restoration. Photo restoration.

Boston Gilding & Framing   (F R)
27 Pine Street
Bedford, MA 01730
617-275-0818
Custom framemaking.

Carl's Frame Shop   (F R)
1907 Rock Castle Park Drive
Valparalso, IN 46383
219-464-2071
Vintage frame restoration.

Carolline's Studio of Restoration (F R A)
24 Byfield Lane
Greenwich, CT 06830
203-661-6340
Antique frames and mirrors. Gilding and decorative painted finishes.

Coleman Fine Art   (F R C)
45 Hasell Street
Charleston, SC 29401
803-853-7000
Framemakers. Restoration and conservation of frames and oils.

Country Frame Gallery   (F R C)
103 Atlantic Avenue
Ocean View, DE 19970
302-539-9193
Regilding and restoration.

Dow Art Gallery   (F R)
3330 Camp Bowie Boulevard
Fort Worth, TX 76107
Gilding, bronzing, and refinishing. Replicate missing ornaments.

Durrett Studio & Gallery (F R A G)
165 North Fairground Street
Marietta, GA 30060
770-424-6039
Sale of period gilt frames. Restoration of antique gilt frames.

Guy E. Downing Art Conservators (F R C)
3500 Takara Road
Chico, CA 95928
916-343-2787
Framemaking, art conservation.

Easter Conservation Services   (F R C)
4502 North Delaware Street
Indianapolis, IN 46205
317-926-5909
Conservators of frames and gilded objects.

Felton Framemaking   (F)
4150 Chelmsford Road
Tallahassee, FL 32308
904-893 -391
Fine custom frames and linen liners.

Field Art Studio   (F R G)
24242 Woodward Avenue
Pleasant Ridge, MI 48069
810-399-1320
Construction of custom frames. Restoration of vintage frames.

The Frame Makers   (F R)
3724 West 19th Street
Tacoma, WA 98466
206-564-2320
Custom- and ready-made frames.

The Gabriel Guild-Miranda Arts (F C G)
6 North Pearl Street
Port Chester, NY 10573
914-935-9362
Custom- and ready-made frames. Conservation of works on paper.

* Gallery of Graphic Arts   (F C G)
1601 York Avenue
New York, NY 10028
212 988 4731
Frames for fabrics of all varieties, including quilts, rugs, banners, flags, Native Indian, beaded; antique and contemporary. Mail order.

Gilding & Frame Restoration Studio (F R C)
7339 Palmetto Street
Philadelphia, PA 19111
215-725-3123
Frames. Restoration of antiques. Conservation.

* Goldfeder\Kahan Framing Group Ltd.   (F C P)
37 West 20th Street
New York, NY 10011
212-242-5310
State-of-the-art custom conservation framing. Clean-room and

environmental climate control ensure museum-quality preservation. Wide variety of moldings. Mail order.

Gold Leaf Conservation   (F C)
624 Golden Oak Pkwy
Cleveland, OH 44146
216-786-1565
Frames. Conservation.

Gold Leaf Frames   (F R C)
470 Atlantic Avenue
Boston, MA 02210
617-426-8650
Frame making and restoration. Conservation.

Gold Leaf Frames of Santa Fe (F C G)
1515 5th Street
Santa Fe, NM 87501
505-988-5005
Gilded frames old and new. Conservation.

Gold Leaf Restoration   (F R)
221 S.E. 11th Street
Portland, OR 97212
503-236-2260
Gild, conserve, and restore all types of frames and objects.

* Gold Leaf Studios   (F C A)
443 "I" Street, N.W.
Washington, D.C. 20001
202-638-4660
Collection of antique frames.
Conservation of gilding and gilded
objects. Interior and exterior
architectural gilding. Mail order
(P.O. Box 50156, Washington, D.C.
20091)

Graybeal Frame & Gilding Company
(F)
1973 Young Road
Chamblee, GA 30341
404-355-4431
Fine custom-made frames

Hartford Framing Company   (F G)
80 Pitkin Street
East Hartford, CT 06108
203-528-1409
Framing and fine art for 100 years.

Husar Picture Frame Company   (F)
1631 West Carroll Avenue
Chicago, IL 60612
312-243-7888
Hand-carved period frames.

Lancaster Galleries   (F R G)
34 North Water Street
Lancaster, PA 17603
717-397-5552
Custom picture framing of craft,
paper, and oils. Frame restoration.

* Andrew Leddy and Company
(F R C A)
1655 Wisconsin Avenue, N.W.
Washington, DC 20007
202-638-5394
Fine 16th–18th century frames,
mirrors, and gilded objects. Frame
conservation. 18th–20th century
hand-crafted frames.

Channing Lefebvre Antique
Restoration   (F R)
904 Park Avenue
Albany, NY 12208
518-489-5960
Antique frames. Restoration
Mayer Studios, Inc.   (F R C)

168 East Market Street
Akron, OH 44308
216-535-6121
Frames. Restorations. Conservation
mounting. Needlework and
shadowboxes. Specialty crating and
shipping.

Mississippi Gold Leaf   (F R A)
P.O. Box 896
Clarksdale, MS 38614
601-624-0575
Restoration and conservation of gilt
frames and furniture. Painted
finishes of the 18th-century.

* Abe Munn*   (F)
51-02 21st Street
Long Island City, NY 11101
718-361-1373
Authentic custom-made antique
reproduction frames, principally in
22K gold leaf.

New York Central II   (F C)
102 Third Avenue
New York, NY 10003
212-420-6060
Custom- and ready-made frames.
Wide variety of moldings. Dry
mounting. Conservation framing.

Oskar's Picture Framing   (F R C)
12 Kellog Road
New Hartford, NY 13413
315-732-7111
Framing. Restoration of antique
frames. Reproduce antique frames
using antique tools.

* Painter's Place   (F)
355 Hayes Street
San Francisco, CA 94102
415-431-9827
Emphasis on custom-designed
contemporary frames.

* J. Pocker & Son   (F C)
135 East 63rd Street
New York, NY 10021
800-782-8434
Custom and conservation framing.
Mirrors and specialty glazing. Search
service. Mail order.

Reed Arts   (F C G)
909 West 5th Avenue
Columbus, OH 43201
614-291-0253
Frames. Conservation and museum
mounting. Figured frames. Paper art
treated for fungus and mildew.

Selected Arts   (F R A G)
9156 Cedros Avenue
Panorama City, CA 91402
818-895-1905
Creative custom frame design.

* The Society of Gilders
P.O. Box 920490
Norcross, GA 30092
770-451-1112
Call or write for a list of members in
your area.

The Stone Studio   (F C)
82 Erskine Road
Stamford, CT 06903
203-322-7018
Specialty is framing works on paper
using conservation methods. Japanese
hinges adhered with wheat paste
starch.

Von Hawk Art Restoration Labs
(F R C)
P.O. Box 546
Paisley, FL 32767
352-669-7776
Restoration of rare art. Frame repair.
Structural analysis of paper art.

Wimsatt & Associates Art
Conservators   (F R C)
4230 Howard Avenue
Kensington, MD 20895
301-493-4250
Conservation of gilded and painted
framed objects and icons. Frame
fabrication and finishing.

ART SUPPLY STORES

Art Supply Warehouse Express
5325 Departure Drive
Raleigh, NC 27604
800-995-6778
Wide range of artist's supplies: mats,

mat cutters, and frames. Mail order.
Catalog.

Daniel Smith
4150 First Avenue South
P.O. Box 84268
Seattle, WA 98124-5568
800-426-6740
Wide variety of do-it-yourself
supplies. Mail order. Catalog.

Dick Blick Art Materials
P.O. Box 1267
Galesburg, IL 61402-1267
800-723-2787
Large selection of ready-made and
section frames for stretched canvases.
Supplies and materials for do-it-
yourself framing. Mail order. Catalog.

Graphik Dimensions Ltd.
2103 Brentwood Street
High Point, NC 27263
800-221-0262
Supplies and materials for do-it-
yourself framing. Mail order. Catalog.

New York Central Art Supply
62 Third Avenue
New York, NY 10003
212-473-7705
Wide selection of conventional and
conservation art papers and boards. A
favorite with students. Mail order.
Catalog.

Pearl Paint Company, Inc.
308 Canal Street
New York, NY 10013-2572
800-221-6845
Custom and ready-made frames.
Frame kits. Wide variety of framing
materials. Conventional and acid-free
mats. Papers and boards. Mail order.
Catalog.

INDEX

A

acrylics, 50
Adam, Robert, 23
aedicular frame, 13, 14, 38
　see also tabernacle frames
agate stone burnisher, 142, 143
altarpieces, 11, 12, 17
aluminum frame, 58–9, 99, 106, 108
antique decorative frame, 95
appliqué, 26
aquatints, 84, 91
arch-topped frame, 42
architectural maps and prints, 88–9
Art Nouveau, 39
artists' prints, 86–7
Arts and Crafts movement, 36 39, 45
assemblages, 100, 101
astragal, 39

B

backgrounds, picture, 164–5
baguette frame, 20, 21, 39, 77
bamboo effect, 91, 97
Barbizon frame, 36
Baroque, 14, 15, 18, 23, 26
bathrooms, 168
beeswax polish, 65
bevel edge, covering the, 129
Biedermeier style, 34, 35
block mounting, 98–9
Bloomsbury Group, 45
blurring technique, 138, 139

body color, 68
bole, 140
bolection frame, 17, 52, 57
Bologna, 12–13
book plates, 91
botanical prints, 93, 96
Braque, Georges, 44
brass corners, 106
brick, bare, 164, 165
British School, 27
burnishing, 142, 143, 147

C

canvas, 50
caricatures, 80
Carlo Maratta style, 23, 24
cartoons and caricatures, 80–81
cartouches, 17, 20
carving, 12, 13, 14, 15
caryatids, 14
cassetta frames, 12, 13, 17, 43
charcoals, 78–9
Chinese paintings, 103
chinoiserie, 25
Chippendale, Thomas, 23, 24, 25
classicism, 14
cleaning, 50, 51
clip frames, 99
cloakrooms, 168
clothing, 110, 111
coins, 115
collage, 100–101
collections, 110, 120
collector (paintings), 160–61
color on color, 133
color photographs, 109
color wash, 132
color washes, 62
combing, 135
combining pictures with objects, 166–7
composition (compo) moldings, 42
concave frame, 52
copper engraving, 84
corner blocks, 32, 36, 42
corridors, 168
costume designs, 82

cracked gesso finish, 144
crackle finish, 91
craft of framing, 124–47
　applied finishes, 144–5
　decorative effects, 134–5
　elaborate frame finishes, 136–7
　gilded frames, 140–43
　making the frame, 130–31
　mat decoration, 128–9
　mats, 126–7
　renovating a frame, 146–7
　simple frame finishes, 132–3
　specialized finishes, 138–9
craquelure finish, 144
crossbanding, 144
crosseted-corner style, 31
Cubism, 44
cuvette frame, 105

D

decorative effects, 134–5
decorative prints, 90–95, 153–4
Degas, Edgar, 40
Delaunay, Robert, 11, 44, 45
Denmark, 35
diptychs, 12, 14
Directoire style, 29
distressing, 142, 143, 147
double mats, 69, 70, 127
dragging, 135
drawings, 76–7
drymounting, 126
Dürer, Albrecht, 11, 68
Dutch metal, 142

E

early prints, 84–5
eaved rooms, 168
Egyptian influence, 26–7, 29
elaborate frame finishes, 136–7
embroidery, 31, 33, 110, 111
Empire style, 26, 27, 28, 29, 35, 36
engravings, 84, 85, 91, 164
ephemera 120–21
equestrian subjects, 64, 65, 154
etching, 84, 85

F

Fabriano paper, 82, 126
fabrics, 82, 110, 112–13, 164–5
fashion prints, 152
flat-effect frames, 52
Flemish frames, 15, 16, 38
France, 17, 18–21, 42, 43
French School, 26
frescoes, 10, 11

G

genre scenes, 91
Germany, 15, 17, 35, 43
Gibbons, Grinling, 22, 24
gilded frames, 140–43
gilded mats, 68
gilding, 13, 17, 26
glass, 67
　nonreflective, 67
Gluck frame, 45
gold frames, 54–7
Gothic influence, 11, 29, 43
gouache, 68, 71
graphic images, 98–9
Greek influence, 26, 29, 37, 38
guilloche pattern, 24, 26
guillotine machine, 130

H

handmade papers, 82, 89, 126
hanging and display, 150–69
　challenges, 168–9
　the collector, 160–61
　combining with objects, 166–7
　different backgrounds, 164–5
　first principles, 152–5
　hanging a single picture, 162–3
　regimented groups, 158–9
　small groups, 156
　hanging a single picture, 162–3
Herrera style, 17
Hicks frame, 31, 33
High Victorian taste, 39
hinged mats, 127

history of framing, 10–45
　American native styles, 30–33
　British developments, 22–5
　the earliest "frames", 11
　the early centuries, 12–17
　French influence, 18–21
　Germany and Scandinavia, 34, 35
　the Impressionists, 40–43
　Neoclassicism, Empire, Regency, 26–9
　the 19th century, 36–9
　the 20th century, 44–5
Hoby frame, 15
Hogarth frame, 25, 85
Holland, 15, 17
hollow frame, 52, 57
Hunt, (William) Holman, 38–9

I

Impressionists, 39, 40, 41, 44
Indian paintings, 102
Indian paper, 82, 126
Ingres paper, 82, 126
inlaid decoration, 26, 31, 34, 35, 77, 94, 103
inscriptions, 16, 32, 36
Italy, 12–13, 17, 38

J

Japanese influence, 33, 39
Japanese paper, 82, 89, 102, 126
Japanese prints, 102
Jugendstil, 39

K

Kent frame, 24, 25
kitchens, 168
Klimt, Gustav, 38, 39
Kneller frame, 24, 25
Kulicke frame, 44

L

lace, 112
landings, 168
landscape paintings, 36, 52
lapis lazuli, 136

Lely frame, 22, 24
Limner frame, 33
lithography, 84, 86, 91, 94
Louis XIII, King, 17, 18, 20, 36
Louis XIV, King, 17, 18, 20, 36
Louis XV, King, 19, 20, 21, 22–3, 40
Louis XVI, King, 11, 19, 20, 21, 26, 29, 40, 157
Lutma frame, 16, 17, 22

M
Mannerism, 14, 25
maps, 88–9
marble strips, 129
marbling, 138, 139
marine subjects, 65, 90, 97
marquetry, 35, 77, 94, 103, 144
mass production, 39, 42, 57
mat decoration, 128–9
mats, 82, 126–7
mezzotints, 84
miniatures, 104–5
mirror makers, 30
mirrors, 14, 15, 18, 21
mixed media, 100–101
Mondrian, Piet, 44
Morris, William, 36, 36, 38, 43
mosaics, 11

N
natural wood frames, 62–3
needleworks, 110, 154, 168
neoclassicism, 20, 23, 24, 26, 28, 29, 33, 35
neo-Impressionists, 39, 44
neoplatonism, 36
nonreflective glass, 67
Northern Europe, 14–15, 17, 28

O
objects and ephemera, 110–21
    ephemera and collections, 120–21
    fabrics, 112–13
    three-dimensional objects, 114–19
oil gilding, 140, 142

oil paintings, tempera and acrylics, 50–65
    aluminum and silver frames, 58–9
    gold frames, 54–7
    natural wood frames, 62–3
    painted frames, 60–61
    the profile of the frame, 52–3
    veneered and dark wood frames, 64–5
    oil paintings, 40, 50–51, 52, 154, 164, 165
oil pastels, 75
oriental work, 102–3
outset corners, 15
oval frames, 107
oval-spandrel frame, 43

P
painted frames, 60–61, 71, 94
painted motifs, 135
Palladianism, 24
panel paintings, 14
paper, works on, 66–109
    architectural prints and maps, 88–9
    artists' prints, 86–7
    cartoons and caricatures, 80–81
    charcoals and pen and ink drawings, 78–9
    collage and mixed media, 100–101
    decorative prints, 90–95
    drawings, 76–7
    early prints, 84–5
    oriental work, 102–3
    pastel paintings, 74–5
    photographs, 106–9
    poster and graphic images, 98–9
    small-scale paintings and miniatures, 104–5
    special treatments, 82–3
    watercolors, 68–73
papier-maché frame, 43
pastel paintings, 74–5
patterned wallpapers, 165

pediments, 12, 13
pen and ink drawings, 78
period frames, 56–7
photographs, 106–9
Picasso, Pablo, 44–5
pickling, 62, 132, 133
pilasters, 12, 13, 14
Pissarro, Camille, 40, 41
plate frame, 52
Plexiglass, 44, 67, 115
pointillisme, 40
porphyry finish, 136, 137
portrait frames, 2, 14–15, 25, 30
portrait photography, 106, 107, 109
posters, 98–9
Pre-Raphaelites, 36, 37, 38, 42
primitive paintings, 97, 138
profile of the frame, 52–3

R
reed and roundel frame, 39
Regence style, 21, 22–3, 27, 28, 29, 35
regimented groups of pictures, 158–9
Renaissance, 12, 14, 39, 43
Renoir, Pierre August, 40
renovating a frame, 146–7
repeat images, 110
reproductions, 57
Restoration, 24
restoration work, 50, 66, 67
ribbon-top frame, 29
rice paper, 102
ripple moldings, 15, 17
Rococo, 19, 20, 21, 22–3, 24, 26, 28, 29, 30
Roman influence, 29
Rome, 12–13
"rope" decoration, 90, 97
rosettes, 24, 26
Rossetti, Dante Gabriel, 36, 38, 39
rounded corner frame, 43

S
Salvatore Rosa-style, 24

Sansovino frame, 14, 15, 17, 22,
Scandinavia, 35
Schinkel frame, 35
Schlag, 142
screen prints, 99
scroll paintings, 102
scrolls, 14, 15
Secessionists, 39, 40
set designs, 82, 83
sets of prints, 92, 93
Seurat, Georges, 40, 45, 79
sgraffito ornament, 17
shadow boxes, 115
Sheraton, Thomas, 27
silver frames, 58–9
silver gilt frames, 142
simple frame finishes, 132–3
slips, 52, 130
small groups of pictures, 156–7
small-scale paintings, 104–5
Spanish frames, 16, 17
special treatments, 82–3
specialized finishes, 138–9
sponging, 136
spoon frame, 52, 57
sporting subjects, 64
stenciling, 30, 31, 35, 96, 97, 135
stepped mats, 69, 70
strapwork, 15, 17
Stuck, Franz von, 38, 39
Sully style, 31
Sunderland frame, 22, 23
Surrealism, 44
Sweden, 34, 35
swept frame, 42

T
tabernacle frames, 12, 13, 14, 38, 39
    see also aedicular frames
tapestries, 110
tarnishing process, 142
tempera, 50
three-dimensional objects, 114–19
tondo frame, 13
topographical prints, 88–9, 153

tortoiseshell-effect frame, 95, 97, 138
triptychs, 12, 14
Tuscany, 12–13

U
underpinner, 130

V
Van Gogh, Vincent, 11, 40
veneered and dark wood frames, 64–5
veneered frames, 144
veneers, 15, 26, 77, 144
Venice, 12–13
verre eglomisé, 88, 92
vignettes, 19
vinegar painting, 30, 35
volutes, 14

W
wallpapers, patterned, 165
washlines, 69–70, 72, 129
water gilding, 140, 142
watercolors, 31, 32, 42, 68–73
Watts frame, 43
wet-mounting, 126
Whistler, James Abbott McNeill, 33, 39, 42, 43
white gold, 142
window mouldings, 30
wood engraving, 84
wood-paneled rooms, 165
woodcuts, 87
woodstains, 133